LANCHESTER LIBRARY

3 8001 00115 1996

WITHDRAWN

D1757838

LANCHESTER LIBRARY — ART & DESIGN LIBRARY
Coventry (Lanchester) Polytechnic
Gosford Street,
Coventry CV1 5RZ

CANCELLED

12 MAR 1997

CANCELLED

16 MAY 2001

14 NOV 2006

This book is due to be returned not later than the
date stamped above. Fines are charged on overdue
books.

PS57298/A

TEAM ZOO

TEAM ZOO

Buildings and Projects 1971–1990

Edited by Manfred Speidel
With contributions by Lucien Kroll,
Manfred Speidel and Patrice Goulet

THAMES AND HUDSON

Translated from the German by Michael Robinson
Translated from the Japanese by Manfred Speidel

Any copy of this book issued by the publisher as a paperback is sold subject to the condition that it shall not by way of trade or otherwise be lent, resold, hired out or otherwise circulated without the publisher's prior consent in any form of binding or cover other than that in which it is published and without a similar condition including these words being imposed on a subsequent purchaser

First published in Great Britain in 1991 by
Thames and Hudson Ltd, London

Copyright © 1991 Verlag Gerd Hatje, Stuttgart

All Rights Reserved. No part of this publication may be reproduced or transmitted in any form or by any means, electronic or mechanical, including photocopy, recording or any other information storage and retrieval system, without prior permission in writing from the publisher

Printed and bound in Germany

COVENTRY POLYTECHNIC
Art and Design Library

Author....TEAM....

Class....724.6 TEA

CONTENTS

EDITOR'S FOREWORD

Japan is still an unknown·country.

Despite the media, despite the closeness fax and television bring, despite thousands of tourists, Japanese businesses abroad and foreign businesses in Japan, the Japanese are and remain an island people; their means of communication make them seem like an impenetrable secret society which the Japanese themselves seem unable or unwilling to open up.

Only a few Japanese personalities have achieved international reputations in the field of architecture. They enjoy the aura of something special, despite the fact that Japan's gigantic building boom and lenient legislation produced an extremely wide range of work. Their greatest merit is individual buildings and their dilemma is urban development.

JA (Japan Architect) and GA (Global Architecture) have produced magnificent volumes of photographs, but only a handful of the younger generation of architects' work has been published outside Japan, attracting attention with a markedly formalistic approach in which architecture is allotted an autonomous role. Perhaps that is easier to understand around the globe than heterogeneous architecture that is milieu-bound and closer to the everyday, but I find the latter more interesting, which is why I made it the focal point of the book and exhibition "Japanische Architektur, Geschichte und Gegenwart" in 1983. The group of architects closest to me personally is Team Zoo.

In the booming, overheated Japanese economy larger contracts naturally do not go to small offices working individually, but to large firms. Their rational working methods guarantee very rapid completion – thus Tokyo town hall, the tallest skyscraper in Japan, was completed in only three years – and a large degree of similarity in appearance.

Small offices fall victim to the enormous presssure of costs, especially because of excessively high rents in cities, and move into the country: for example, Itsuko Hasegawa has moved to a deserted farmhouse on the island of Awajishima, and Atelier Zō to a school building on the island of Hokkaido. Typically their contracts come largely from the provinces as well.

Team Zoo's Atelier Iruka built an acclaimed primary school in the city of Izushi, which is under protection as a town of outstanding historical interest. The school's distinctive features are room and group layouts corresponding to individual age groups and a lavish roofscape appropriate to the setting. This produced another commission for a school from a little town on the island of Awajishima because they too did not want some sort of elegant box. This is pleasing, but no cause for optimism when one sees how urban and rural landscapes are so mercilessly destroyed by new buildings elsewhere.

I hope that readers of this book will be able to use the pictures to make a voyage of discovery to a Japan that can arouse curiosity and understanding when artists like Team Zoo work in a way completely related to milieu and site, entirely from within themselves.

This publication attempts to present a cross-section of the group's highly varied work. We have restricted ourselves to projects by architectural offices within Team Zoo, and had to leave out groups working in the town planning field.

The most important work by the founder members of Team Zoo came in the early days. The first summary of their notions of space and form is "Alphabet", a contribution to an exhibition in the USA in 1978. Unfortunately only part of this could be reproduced. Again only single examples were chosen of the series of kindergartens by Atelier Mobile and the large number of park and landscape designs by Atelier Zō, and the many detached houses built by the Iruka Studio, to give an impression of the many ideas involved, and the ways in which they were transformed and developed. It did not prove possible to include work by the Ryū group, which has only been working independently since 1989; in the mean time they have completed an extension for a design school in Tokyo, and several residential buildings.

An overall presentation including all groups and projects would not fit into the framework of a single book. In order to give an idea of the size of the individual offices, lists of studios and their employees have been provided, and a select bibliography for those in search of further information.

I should like to thank Akira Hasegawa, Ulla Lytton, Alexander Maul, Gabi Palm and Philipp Schödel for translation work, and Peter Krebs for various drawings.

Manfred Speidel

JAPAN TODAY

Lucien Kroll

I went to Japan for the first time as a guest of the "New Towns as Human Heritage" congress organized by the new town of Senri, near Osaka.

Like everybody else I was aware of the terrible contrasts in this country, between feudalism replaced by incomprehensible militarism that ended in a débâcle, and a gentle way of life, domestic precision, austerity of milieu and customs, profoundly regional culture, tragic or comic poetry and very tender music. All the clichés in other words, and I couldn't find them reflected in the hard images created by either the heroic architects of contemporary Japan, or by the victorious industries, which one could suspect of having taken over the military baton.

I did however find a peaceful people, very reassuring, ceremonious and extraordinarily friendly (if they were sincere...?). I successfully avoided large-scale international architecture and plunged into the alleyways to size up the acute sense of small spaces, their organization, their decoration and their amiability. I saw a spontaneous creativity that I thought modern architects and industrial prefabricators had obliterated. And the great national tradition of organized, overpopulated, interdependent and amiable promiscuity.

They are at last getting out of the habit of rebuilding their entire country at the slightest hint of fire or earthquake, they are starting to learn to resist the temptation. They do rebuild their temples every twenty years. "If we didn't," they say, "time wears them out, and we would forget what they were like." Nevertheless galloping urbanization and property speculation are currently destroying more than the earthquakes ever did...

I was able to check up on the continuity of this tradition through architecture, the teaching of Takamasa Yoshizaka, and his now mature students' projects, particularly those of Team Zoo, its founders and their successors. These projects take up the popular tradition very directly, its organization, forms and above all its materials, from a completely contemporary point of view and with a formal freedom that can never resist a humourous touch.

It was decided that 1987 should be Le Corbusier year, and this provoked tides of unduly insipid praise, and excessively violent criticism. But little was written on Le Corbusier's admitted or non-admitted "descendants", and particularly not on Yoshizaka, his independent view of Le Corbusier, his teaching and above all the generations of students trained by him, who have abandoned Le Corbusier's precepts, but retained a tinge of them.

The fact is that magazines and colleges only talk about Le Corbusier's prewar trainees, in the period when he was preaching "machinisme", who successfully built large living machines. There is little talk of Yoshizaka, who fortunately knew Le Corbusier only after the war, in a gentler and more civilized period.

Some of Yoshizaka's students got together and founded Team Zō. They have worked and expanded all over Japan.

Tsutomu Shigemura, one of the founder members, is director of Atelier Iruka in Kobe, and took me to see the library he has just finished at Wakimachi, on the island of Shikoku. Near Osaka, he said: train to the boat, which takes an hour and a half, then another train, then a bus. We came back by plane, which was quicker... The distances are crazy.

Traditional shop in Wakimachi

Here then is a "normal" project: he has taken careful account of the old town in which he was going to build. He refused to demolish the old disused warehouses to make room for an imposing cubic building. He insinuated himself between them, and continued the scale and spatial organization of the village without a break, its formal and structural diversity, exterior colour, materials and their use.

And it is not pastiche. He integrated roofs and old walls that could still be used into his architecture naturally, so that the joins between old and new could not be seen. All this is of course

Roof ornaments in Wakimachi

conceived using methodical design and modern building methods.

Nevertheless these rational tools remain simple devices, content to help to execute a form of architecture created to affirm milieu and culture, rather than building methodology: "high-tech" has certainly always been a kind of morbid abuse of contemporary techniques, but they do not need be demonstrated so romantically and with such brutality.

Then we paid a visit to a little tile factory which he had helped to survive by commissioning it to make the birds and traditional dragons used on roof ridges for him. The exterior walls have been reclad using the old plastering method; because it is compressed it becomes very resistant and moistureproof. He found old craftsmen who had been forgotten to an extent: they trained young apprentices, thus assuring the future of the tradition.

Street in Wakimachi on the backside of the library

The village texture continues in a passage leading to the inner library courtyard, and especially in the organization of the interior spaces and the design of the furniture, which has the same urbane complexity as the exterior.

The operation sits so amiably in an urban texture of this quality, continuing its past towards a peaceful future, it is linked with the economy of local trades, it is rooted to this extent in the character of the place, it is articulated in complex spaces, and so for all these reasons it certainly qualifies as very contemporary architecture. And incidentally, it is admirably designed.

TEAM ZOO, TAKAMASA YOSHIZAKA AND LE CORBUSIER

Manfred Speidel

Prologue

I went to Japan in April 1968. I had a grant and wanted to spend an additional year at Waseda University in Tokyo studying architecture – Japanese architecture.

Actually I didn't want to go to Waseda, I would have preferred the University of Tokyo. Kenzo Tange taught there. His wonderful sports halls for the Olympic Games were built in 1964; the mysterious curves of their roofs had written in the sky a tension-charged figure that had never been seen before. In chaotic Tokyo they were shapes from an exotic world with a particular feeling for magnificent form. I felt that Kunio Maekawa's 1961 Ueno concert hall came from that world as well. It is opposite Le Corbusier's little museum building, and under the broad unfolding of its concrete roof between the two concert halls creates the feeling of an urban square inside, something that was particularly missing in Tokyo. I often drank coffee on the terrace.

I went to Professor Takamasa Yoshizaka at Waseda University. Who was Yoshizaka? Lean, powerful head, Ho Chi Minh beard, thick glasses; Yoshizaka was always in buttoned sports shirt, no tie, listening, terse replies, curious; it made me uneasy, a man who always stood current notions and views on their head, who had travelled all over the world and climbed some of its highest mountains.

The April issue of Japan Architect had just published a piece of work completed by him and his U-Ken design group: the Inter University Seminar House outside Tokyo – huts, spread around a shorn hill, plywood huts with slightly vaulted roofs, arranged in groups, and an inverted concrete pyramid pegged into the hill above.

I found the whole thing very diffuse and simply ugly, it had no complete, unified form, it wasn't a clearly formulated piece of architecture, a structure that should have been pleasing to the eye, and to the photographic eye as well – compared, for example, with the curved and imposing giant slabs of the huge residential buildings in Tokyo Bay, designed by Tange. I could not find anything here to correspond with my sense of beauty, my ideas of architecture – and I intended to study here? I didn't stay for one year in the end, I stayed for almost ten. I first visited Yoshizaka's Seminar Village after two years. The hill was now covered with trees and bushes. I was surprised. I felt a sense of well-being, as though I had arrived in a little Italian mountain village! The architecture had become part of nature and – part of the human beings.

I had experienced something that I could not put into words, that affected me and that made this simple little village seem equal in value to the brilliant monuments built by Tange and Maekawa, and able to stand alongside Kikutake's and Maki's intellectual constructions. Why was this? The built-up hill looked as though it had been worked on by a fool. I was alarmed by its playful nonseriousness; it wasn't easy to entrust myself to this. But there was something else, between the buildings, something that gave

a stay there the feeling of a "beautiful use" (Bruno Taut), without it being possible to trace this phenomenon back to the buildings as such.

The complex made me perceive the place, the hill upon which it stood, as something splendid, and I found the people assembled there, in the spatial relationships the buildings endowed them with, immensely pleasant.

Later, in 1975, Yoshizaka coined the concept of "method through discovery", "hakkenteki hoho" for this way of working. Discovery was an emancipatory first step in planning. I asked Yoshizaka to introduce it here in Germany. He died on 16 December 1981 at the age of 64, on the day he intended to give a lecture in Aachen. Yoshizaka himself had handed the planned lecture over to his pupil Tsutomu Shigemura, who had been one of the most important research members of the Yoshizaka group while he was at university. But Shigemura was also one of the founder members of Team Zō, formed in 1971 by a group of pupils and colleagues of Yoshizaka. In 1983 Shigemura and I planned and designed the "Japanese Architecture. Past and Present" exhibition in Düsseldorf. My personal relationship with Yoshizaka and Team Zoo (as the various groups are now called) must make my remarks seem very biased, and I am happy for them to be seen as such in this essay. But I am convinced that it is important to start a book about Team Zoo with an article about Takamasa Yoshizaka.

Yoshizaka was born on 23 February 1917 in Tokyo. The family was in Geneva from 1929 to 1933, where the father was in the diplomatic service. Takamasa Yoshizaka graduated from Waseda University in Tokyo in 1941, and joined the staff there in 1946. From 1950 to 1952 he worked with Le Corbusier in Paris. He was given a chair at Waseda University in 1954 and founded an architectural office under the name U-Ken.

Important buildings and plans include:

1956	Japanese pavilion at the Venice Biennale
	Ura house, Ura-tei, in Kobe
1957	Villa Coucou, Tokyo
1958	Kaisei Gakuin school, Nagasaki
1959	Maison Japonaise, Tokyo
1961–2	Kureha school, Toyama
	Athené Française, Tokyo; Gozu town hall
1965, 1969	Plans and buildings for reconstruction of Oshima Island, Tokyo
1965–6, 1969	Inter University Seminar House, Hachioji near Tokyo
1969	Aeronautical Museum, Ikomayama near Nara,
1970	Competition: "Japan in the 21st Century".

Further important events:

1971	A group from U-Ken – Keiko Arimura, Hiroyasu Higuchi, Koichi Otake, Tsutomu Shige-

mura and Reiko Tomita – founded an architectural office of their own: Team Zō (elephant). This came about as a result of commissions for the Okinawa Islands, which had been returned to Japan; they built houses.

1972–81 Yoshizaka and U-Ken: several smaller buildings, additions to Inter University Seminar House, town plannings; most important theoretical work.

From 1975 For Team Zō there were so many town planning and architectural commissions and the group had become so big that they organized themselves into "Ateliers", which loosely formed "Team Zoo": the original core was Atelier Zō (Elephant); the other groups are called Atelier Gaii (Bull), Atelier Iruka (Dolphin), Atelier Ryū (Dragon), Atelier Kujira (Whale), Atelier Kuma (Bear), Atelier Mobile (Running Bird), Atelier Todo (Sea Lion), Atelier Wani (Crocodile), Atelier 140.

1981 Death of Takamasa Yoshizaka.

1982–6 Yoshizaka's former pupils and colleagues published his writings and buildings in seventeen volumes. They contain an enormously voluminous body of theory.

Yoshizaka's buildings take Le Corbusier's prototypical architectural designs, which had been the basis of his and many Japanese architects' work since the mid thirties, when Maekawa and Sakakura returned from Le Corbusier's studio, and "broke them up". Yoshizaka brought them to life with his ethnographical cast of mind, brought them to life in and for Japan. For his pupils Yoshizaka became a rich source of unorthodox thinking and unusual architectural images. I should like to present some of these in this article.

Creating a place

A path with very shallow, broad steps leads up from the main thoroughfare into a little wood, as if going to a mysterious place. The path reaches a point of rest at a little circle of stone slabs with

Takamasa Yoshizaka. Japanese Pavilion at the Venice Biennale. 1956 (1-3)

a low wall and then turns right at an acute angle. There, in a clearing in the woods, is a simple, completely closed building raised above the ground, and the path leads to a bridge-like flight of steps, to the entrance of the mysterious treasure-house.

2

Just before the steps, at the foot of an old pine tree, a spring bubbles up from a little mound by a stone. From this a little brook cuts its way under the steps and along the building to its rear, where it disappears as a fine waterfall in a thin thread into the cave-like space under the building.

3

The path climbing up through the wood, the clearing with the spring and the little rivulet cutting through the ground create an intense feeling of a place that could be holy.

The four stilts, which carry the building like a holy storehouse that is not allowed to touch the floor because it contains valuable treasures, signal the respect with which this man-made building was placed in its natural surroundings, while at the same time giving form to those surroundings.

What I have just described is not the entrance to a shrine of nature in Japan, but to the Japanese Pavilion at the Venice Biennale, built in 1956 by Takasama Yoshizaka and Juichi Otake.

This description may not be quite correct: you actually pass one side of the building and go through under a corner of it before going into the wood. But my words reproduce my first surprised experience when I was looking for the Japanese pavilion for the first time at the Venice Biennale, among the other countries' buildings, which were all facing the main thoroughfares.

Takamasa Yoshizaka. Japanese Pavilion
at the Venice Biennale. 1956

As he wrote himself[1], Yoshizaka took over the idea of a closed
box raised on stilts from Le Corbusier, the core of his museum
that grew in a spiral, called "boîte à miracles"[2], box of miracles,
by Le Corbusier. Le Corbusier used the stilts, known as pilotis,
to raise buildings off the ground, to make them separate, but the
space gained under the building remained neutral, available and
empty, and was not given a shape of its own within the topography: an old photograph of the Swiss House in the Cité Univer-
sitaire in Paris shows two students sitting somewhere on the
uncomfortable platform under the building on chairs they have
brought themselves; in the Villa Savoye the open space between
the pilotis is an access point and parking space for cars, and
under La Tourette the stilts form a non-spatial escape route. Only
a few architects of the Modern movement, like Hans Scharoun
for example, have used topography as an unambiguous fixed
point for their buildings and thus continued the land formation in
and through the building. Frank Lloyd Wright's house Falling
Water is the most spectacular reshaping of a dramatic, natural
place that is further enhanced by the architecture. It seems as
though the "obstruction" posed by the waterfall could "only" be
conquered and transformed into usable land by the surfaces
protruding one above the other like cascades.

This reminds me of a passage from the Sakuteiki, the 12th
century Japanese garden treatise, where instructions are given on
how one can create the impression that a building had been

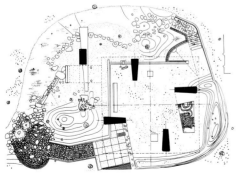

Takamasa Yoshizaka. Japanese Pavilion. 1956
Ground plan of the site under the pilotis

constructed on a difficult natural site and then became an
inextricable part of it:

"If someone is trying to create the impression of a mountain
village, it could be made interesting in the following manner:

"He must set a high hill next to the building and spread a few
stones from the top of the hill down to its foot.

"It should look as though, to build the house, he had to dig away
one side of the hill, and that while levelling the site, a large,
natural stone appeared, and was uncovered. As it was rooted
very deeply, and impossible to dig out and take away, a pillar of
the house was based upon it, after this pillar had been shaped to
fit the stone."[3]

This is precisely Yoshizaka's idea and method. The spring and
little mound by his pavilion are artificial. They mark the artifi-
cially created edge of the site as if they had been there first, and
the building had to fit in with them. Building and land create a
space of their own under the building, intended for showing
sculpture at the exhibition. Entrance, approach, building and
land form a kind of spatial junction that is open and permeable.
This formal relationship of building to land is given meaning in
Eastern Asia by the notion of the earth as a dragon whose veins
must not be injured.

A building is not permitted to hinder the passage of currents of
energy arising from land and water formations, but rather it
should relate to them in such a way that man can participate in
them without being destroyed by them.

A tension arises between a feeling of being hidden in the
hollows, protected by the rise, and a feeling of breadth, where
the site opens up for the eye.

Junzo Sakakura. Museum of Modern Art,
Kamakura. 1951

Junzo Sakakura, who worked with Le Corbusier in the thirties,
also used his basic museum type for the Museum of Modern Art
in Kamakura, 1951: he too, in the same sense as Yoshizaka,
transformed the area under the pilotis into a protected space
connected with the pool by which the buildings stands, from
which the eye glides dreaming into the distance over the water.
In subsequent buildings Yoshizaka further dramatized the relationship with the site. He placed buildings against a steep slope
and made increased difficulty of access into a special experience.

The Gozu town hall building (1962) is designed like a two-storey
bridge, with its head sitting in a hill and its arm held high over the
levelled site. The main entrance for the public is placed at the
point at which the splayed supports hold the arm of the bridge. A

ridge of the hill crest ends in front of the building in a mound of stones piled up in a cone shape. The path leads on to the cone in a spiral, and a footbridge leads across to the entrance. Tension is created by the building, which seems to be unreachable, and its isolation is "only" broken up by the skilful use of the natural site. Yoshizaka was a passionate mountaineer, and his experiences have taken on architectural form.

Takamasa Yoshizaka. Gozu town hall. 1962

The main building of the Inter University Seminar House in Hachioji is in the form of a pyramid standing on its tip, plugged into the hill like a wedge. The top of the hill is only slightly damaged by the small base, and the structure with its curved skin roof completes the silhouette of the hill.
The mound left at the side of the main building is so high that from it one can get into the upper storey – as if into a castle – across a narrow bridge. It spans the abyss dramatically. The feeling of dizziness as one crosses it is heightened by the fact that the building banks steeply inwards, and this takes away any feeling of being firmly anchored.

Takamasa Yoshizaka and U-Ken. Inter University Seminar House, Hachiōji. 1966

From Europe, I should like to quote Mario Botta's ideas on the relationship between architecture and place, although his designs are more like confrontations or delimitations of landscape or an existing settlement.
In his lecture "Architecture and Environment", 1978, he states that he is aware that a building is an intervention into an existing structure and is thus in principle a "disturbance", but that in this way it becomes part of a greater context, which it influences in its turn. Three different attitudes are usual here: adaptation, dominance or transformation.

Takamasa Yoshizaka and U-Ken.
Inter University Seminar House,
Hachiōji. 1966. Main building

The first two produce no artistic statement – an architectural work of art cannot be created either by paralysis or by domination: "It cannot be a matter of preserving landscape and surroundings, but of transformation, with the building as the means to this end." It is a matter of "setting in motion and making easier a different structuring of the" historical and landscape "values of the place, so that today's demands can be fulfilled and man's relationship with his environment can be brought into new equilibrium."
Yoshizaka's buildings create precisely such transformations, but more dramatically than Botta can achieve with his aesthetic commitment.
Landscape and building are and remain a mutual disturbance, an intervention that remains detectable in the exaggeration of topography to abyss and summit, but which at the same time makes the building absolute, and turns it into a spatial and three-dimensional place, just accessible on fragile footbridges, as in designs by Ledoux.
New experiences are opened up. Yoshizaka makes the contrast between the works of man and nature conscious, and uses the shock as a starting point. Architecture becomes a place of refuge, and as a work of art draws its meaning from this.

From place to architecture as landscape
Team Zoo built on these ideas, but in a more conciliatory form. Many of their buildings form a landscape, they are pieces of built topography in places where the landscape is unformed. At the town hall and community centre in Miyashiro-cho, Tochigi (1980), the most important place and the greatest surprise in the faceless, completely flat little town is the large, green rising arena formed as a space and artificial hilly landscape by the gallerylike building. When in the course of time street side and roof become a great overgrown vineyard, from which only a row of arches looks out, the impression will be of a fairy-tale Sleeping Beauty's castle on a hill covered with soft grass, in the rampant undergrowth of which the architecture reveals the wonders of spatial art as a clear structure made by the hand of man.

From uniformity to richness in unity
Space that can be remembered

The interior of the Biennale pavilion is very impressive. It has four closed walls with the entrance door as the only opening, a square ground plan and four broad pillars placed symmetrically in the ground plan to form a swastika pattern. Each of the four pillars supports a girder on which six concrete beams rest, protruding from the girder with one long and one short arm. Light is admitted through glass bricks between the beams. The ceiling is like a "brise-soleil". A dark square left in the middle, with a small square through which light falls on to the square on the floor, which can be opened downwards.

A simple ground plan, the pillars which look like wall fragments that structure the space into four niches turning round the centre, top light through the beams as the only source, all this gives a sequence from simple and closed, down below, to articulated and open, up above, from a peaceful background to the works of art to the lavish ornament of the beam structure, from a well proportioned space that can be immediately grasped on entering to the unfolding of the multiple form of its parts when one stays for a time. All the parts function simultaneously for the purpose of exhibition, structure and décor.

Japanese Pavilion. Interior

Le Corbusier did not manage to produce a space that was so dynamic and at the same time so unified in his museum in Tokyo, although the basic spiral would lead one to expect that. He used round columns, creating a neutral space in and under the building, which can be divided by screens as wished. He followed the doctrine of independent structure and ground plan, which brings about mutual disturbance. In the 1955 Jaoul buildings he had bound his spatial form to the supporting longitudinal walls. Covering this order by breaking up the walls gives a pleasant release of tension while retaining the unity of the elements that make up the space.

With his four free-standing pillars arranged like a swastika Yoshizaka creates a frozen swirl of space in the neutral box, a dynamic spatial and structural picture from which the ground plan is formed: four intimate spatial sections for displaying works of art emerge of their own accord between the pillars and the outer walls.

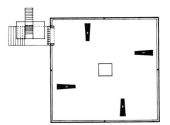

Japanese Pavilion. Ground plan

Surprise in Le Corbusier's museum is created only by disrupting the system – a prismatic opening with a skylight in the ceiling diagonal to the main axes transforms the support with the ceiling open above it into a sculpture relating to the intersecting beams, which, clearly exposed for a time, then disappear in the neutral ceiling again.

The exhibition rooms are then fairly boring. The low ceiling strip leaves room for bands of high windows, but the central division makes the space oppressive.

Yoshizaka experiments with multiform continuous spaces within simple volumes and with unity of spatial form and structure.

After going over the bridge to the main building of the Inter University Seminar Village the visitor slips through a small hole in the wall and a room with stairs leading up and down appears before him. The spatial dividers are as oblique as the outer wall. The pyramid is a large, continuously articulated hollow space with slanting planes and the stairs as a backbone, as if in a great snail shell.

We are familiar with images of rooms like this from fairy tales or dreams. The rooms are closed and yet extend endlessly under stairs and foot-bridges, like Piranesi's Carceri; they are exciting ideal images, signalling primeval experiences.

Inter University Seminar House. Main building. Interior

Inter University Seminar House.
Choki seminar building. 1968–69

But Yoshizaka also associates certain kinds of communal living with continuous spaces of this kind. This was clear to me when I visited the Choki Building (1968/1969) in the Inter University Seminar Village. The square ground plan is divided into four, and the quarters rise around a central core, each time a quarter of a storey higher, forming an open spiral tower in which the students live. Two squares are placed next to each other, intersecting within a quarter of the space: this is the communal space, containing wash-basins for the group. A feeling of pleasant tension is produced as you climb up; the combination of continuous open space of which only a part can be seen at any given time, with sleep and study areas for one person divided off from each other by displaced levels, makes it possible to be together, but with everyone in his own little world, without being completely cut off from the others.

A memorable room must have a quality of complex simplicity and contain an archetypal idea. Le Corbusier sowed the seed for this. He found multiplicity of form and freedom by retrospective articulation of simple figures. The Yoshizaka group wanted to find a creative principle for articulating space so that it can provide several things at once: striking spatial form, function, construction and a definition of the relationship of individual and group.

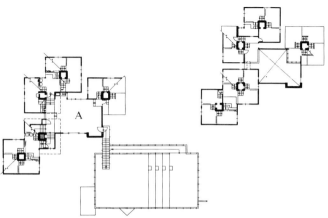

Inter University Seminar House. Choki seminar building. Ground plan

From continous to discontinuous unity

Le Corbusier tried out a spatial principle that Yoshizaka and his pupils made central to their work: in his late period Le Corbusier created a space by joining together sections shaped in different ways, without giving them customary structural forms, or unifying and harmonizing them in rectangular buildings: this was the church at Ronchamp (1950–1954).

The notion of "discontinuous unity", putting together heterogenous individual parts, emerged with Yoshizaka's design for the Seminar Village. Team Zō took this literally and developed it. The Domo Serakanto, built in 1974, is a house christened "coelacanth" because of its shape, created within a long, heterogeneous group process: five members of the team designed individual sections, which was allowed to show in the clear joints within the completed building. They gain unity from the image of the fish.

"The coelacanth crawled out from the sea, with its gills, spine, horn, cilium, teeth, antennae and scales it appeared in the wind and sank in the light. A fish dreaming about architecture an architecture dreaming about fish."[4]

This sounds like dissolution, anarchy – new images and impertinent, unrestrained transposition. Team Zō had discovered that teamwork, even when markedly individual, can still produce a coherent whole, if a common image exists that each individual can interpret differently, and that allows a great deal of scope.

Surely Ronchamp is also monstrously animal-like in its appearance and mysteriously allegorical, in that it is intended to be a cave on top of a hill? Surely there is something in the heterogeneous composition that derives from Le Corbusier's 1920 paintings? There everyday items are put together, individual objects that do not directly cohere in either form or content – violin, book, pipe, bottle, only held together by positions on a surface that determine proportions, and by the table as a frame.

"Serakanto" was a playful poeticization to describe a single, heterogeneous shape. Tsutomu Shigemura retained this particular artistic approach for the library in the well-preserved old town of Wakimachi. Here historical and modern forms are placed side by side, historical where the new building is directly adjacent to existing buildings, thus forming a complete image with them, and new where there is no direct contact with older substance. Some of the new forms are again transformations of existing motifs.

This juxtaposition of different forms gives a strange crispness and freshness, and allows a stimulating oscillation between nostalgic harmony with the surroundings and new sensuality in building.

From discontinuous unity to large-scale form

In the Culture Centre in Miyashiro-cho, Atelier Zō threw a great cloak over the irregular patchwork of the individual rooms, a large-scale form arising from the rectangular external shape of the plot and the semi-circle of the arena, placed off-centre inside. Both external and internal shapes are made up of arches, so that in between – as with a loose-fitting garment – there is air, an open, splendid space to walk about in. The loose-fitting garment offers more possibilities than skin-tight jeans, and gives shape to the faceless town around it.

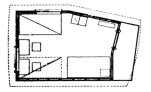

Inter University Seminar House.
Seminar hut. Basic unit

From rationalistic large-scale form to group form

In Yoshizaka's Choki seminar building, two intersecting squares form a pair with a communal space, the junction with wash-basins, two and a half pairs are placed around a room between them, a seminar room (A). The units that can be added can form groups because they have a bit missing. This missing bit is the common section of the pairs, and in between the pairs is the common part of the group. Because of their incompleteness, despite all their individuality, they are able to form a group. For me it was an astonishing discovery to see that the experience of living together can be transferred to architecture as well, and that this in its turn supports the particular way of life.

Le Corbusier's villa type with garden, shown as "Pavillon de l'Esprit Nouveau" at the Paris Exposition des Arts Décoratifs in 1925, is a cut-out rectangle, with the cut-out section as a garden courtyard. This design is well suited to large-scale series and stacks, as in the "Immeubles Villas". A simple form is chosen so that units can be put together to form an aesthetic whole.

Adolf Behne identified this intention very clearly in his book *Der Moderne Zweckbau* in 1926, and formulated it very precisely: rationalists – and Le Corbusier is their most succinct representative – are concerned to stress the whole by assembling parts in sequence; joining together (identical) sections places them in a relationship that emphasizes community, it contains an element of play. Play presupposes community, order and rules. Le Corbusier: "The goal of man's building will is unification."

Functionalists, so Behne observes, plan buildings from the inside out, and only appeal to individuals not attracted to community life. For rationalists community is the most important thing. They try to find the most suitable solution for general needs, the norm, most fitting for a large number of cases. The result is a simple form that can be replicated. Of course it cannot be proved that only simple form can be replicated, and Behne notes the danger of the "rationalist" reduction method: play can easily become a (military) parade, a constraint.[5] This is where Yoshizaka comes in. Optimized joining together without gaps does produce a whole, but not necessarily a group or community. But in the case of the Inter University Seminar Village he is concerned with community and group formation. He changes Le Corbusier's abstract type that can be replicated into an individual item that can be replicated and function in a group. This is yet another approach to put alongside those of the rationalists and functionalists.

In the rectangular, two-person-hut, the standard building in the village, one side is slightly cut back and the front pushed inwards a little. If huts are added along the capped side, a curve is produced, and if they are added along the straight side, a zig-zag line. This creates different group forms within the undulating formation on the hill.

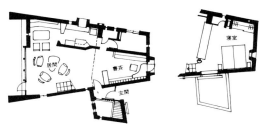

Takamasa Yoshizaka. Villa Coucou. Tokyo, 1957. Ground plan

Takamasa Yoshizaka. Villa Coucou, Tokyo. View

Cutting back individual elements makes it possible when creating a sequence to produce, quite informally, a communal open space within the group, and it is not until this is done that the group is defined. I see the beginning of this formal development in the 1957 Villa Coucou. It began as a breaking open of Le Corbusier's Citrohan-type scheme for a particular situation in Tokyo.

Hans Scharoun's 1951 Darmstadt school design was based on a similar concept. Classrooms give spatial experiences in different forms corresponding to the three age groups, joined together in

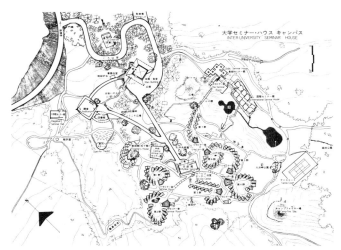

Inter University Seminar House. Ground plan of complete complex

different arrangements: self-contained for the younger children, or as rooms set on the communal route through the school for the older ones.

The symbol for Yoshizaka's image of a group is not a complete, closed circle but two hands held close together, rounded but not touching. This expresses a half-open group. The form clearly defines the community, but does not cut it off from others. Even with clear separation from the immediate environment, there are points at which it is open. The school built in Kureha in 1960 is conceived in this way. It has classroom buildings with three arms and two half-moon-shaped special classrooms, forming a half-open double group. Further groups could be created by the addition of further classroom elements with three arms.

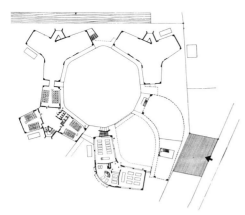

Takamasa Yoshizaka and U-Ken. School in Kureha. 1960. Ground plan

Yoshizaka not only left the figure open, he also distorted the circle as an ideal form. Logical group form would be a circle, so that everybody can see everybody else. In the Seminar Village the parts of the circle are displaced to form a spiral, or the elements lined up in straight sections. A perfect circle would have a centre, and this could suggest compulsion and control. Instead of this the huts are placed tangentially to an imagined centre formed by them. It looks more like an accumulation around a centre than a concentration on it. The community is prestructured, but not uniformly shaped. For the eye this is confusing, and the effect is not beautiful; but if you live there for a few days you enjoy this informality in the group.

Scharoun was thinking in a similar way when he arrived at the shape for the Philharmonie in Berlin, which also gives the visitor

Takamasa Yoshizaka and U-Ken. School in Kureha

Inter University Seminar House.
Seminar group

a feeling of community. Not all the groups of seats face the orchestra directly, but include a view of other members of the audience. Meeting and seeing other people as part of a greater community is as important as the best possible acoustics and orientation towards the music. In Scharoun's design the social utopia of the 1919 "concept of people's house" is still present.

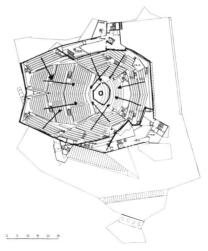

Hans Scharoun. Philharmonie in Berlin

In Alvar Aalto's spatial structures individual parts touch an imaginary centre as well, standing around it like the ribs of an open fan. They are figures of liberation, bound by energy, directed towards a real or imaginary centre. I should again like to cite an image from Japanese garden theory that captures this kind of association. In a set of instructions for grouping stones, larger groups of stones are described as if they were interactive living creatures:

"Stones lying at the foot of a mountain or in the fields seem like a group of village dogs lying down, or like a herd of pigs running in different directions, or like calves romping around with their mothers."[6]

These images describe the group dynamic of individuals striving towards a nearby or distant goal, or related to each other. As

第五十八図 家の走りちられるが如し

Illustration from the Sakuteiki. "A herd of pigs running in different directions"

applied in the Seminar Village this notion can quite clearly be perceived as both a way of bringing people together and a relief from this. The group is half open, the units, the "individuals", incomplete – the huts have only table and bed, the washbasins are communal facilities in the open air that again offer the possibility of communication.

Le Corbusier's villas are also "incomplete". In the villa block there is a large-scale relief kitchen and centralized provision procurement; cleaning is by a "service team". These are neutral institutions bringing what is wanted to the door. The lack of something is not made into a means of communication, as with Yoshizaka, but the services guarantee comfort in the context of isolated, undisturbed privacy. Le Corbusier's image of community is one of individuals living in close proximity but completely cut off from each other, meeting at most on the sports field or at the cinema. His image is that of the Carthusian monastery with tiny holes for provisions in the cloister that do not disturb the monks' isolation behind their never-open doors. It is the image of the hermit in a supply co-operative without any wish for community. "A student wants a well-lit and well-heated monk's cell with a corner from which he can watch the stars. He wants to be within two paces of the place where he can play sport with his friends. His cell should be quite selfcontained, to the extent that this can possibly be achieved."[7]

Yoshizaka's university life is one of a free community of pupils and teachers, made up of individuals with character and abilities who are incomplete, who need each other in order to create anything major. The groups of huts isolated from the outside world have their counterpart in the large community building, which dominates the hill and represents the village to the outside world. Bath-house, cafeteria, library and the larger seminar rooms have mediatory functions and are placed between them. The buildings, their place and functions are conceived to reflect human behaviour and human characteristics as seen by Yoshizaka: introverts, extroverts, and the people who mediate between them. They are only complete together, externally perhaps a group that seems unordered, made up of mutually complementary and different abilities. There is no sign of aspiring to perfection. Community can only grow in imperfection. The little groups organize themselves, only the community needs organizational help like timetables, for example. In the Seminar Village Yoshizaka was trying to create a place for university life outside strictly regulated society in which community, *communitas*, is possible.

For him, exactly as for Lucien Kroll after 1968, universities were intended to be islands in society in which a utopia of equality, of

informal, selfdetermining community would be possible as a basis for the development of personality and where creative human beings could unfold.

The conditions for such a community would be forms of living together in the same way, where same does not mean precisely alike, but egalitarian, i. e. without privileges for the few, but with possibilities or various ways of living together. Simplicity is a prerequisite for equality, and groups must be self-organizing to operate as communities. Privacy is not unqualifiably good. A social anti-structure of this kind (Victor Turner)[8] only stresses the natural differences of its members in terms of their abilities, character and the size of the group, which should all be complementary.

In traditional cultures such anti-structures are set up for periods of initiation. For Yoshizaka and Kroll the university is one of the few places in the modern world where an ideal society of this kind can be realized during a certain period of transition, where a constrained society can provide missing life forms that continue to be effective despite it.

Lucien Kroll's student buildings in Brussels house different group forms alongside each other: communes, individual and intermediate forms with single rooms and large communal rooms. Public paths and terraces lead through the buildings, and external steps run close to the private areas. The present generation of students is looking for isolation again, however, as can be seen from the locked doors and bells in the corridors.

Yoshizaka's Seminar Village and Kroll's student halls of residence both represent an irritation to classical notions of architecture; perhaps they are also too deeply committed to the group idea, too tied to life to be able to be harmonious works of art.

From group form to community form

Team Zoo returns to unification, to overall architectural design, without falling back on Le Corbusier's puritanical prototypes. The school in Miyashiro-cho shows both aspects, large-scale form – broken up – and group form – open on one side and sternly closed on the town side. The simple arrangement of classrooms on an outer corridor is interrupted by glazed bays for each classroom, forming a connection with the other classes. The transitional roofs from yard to corridor, under which shoes are taken off, provide each class with its own passage, its entrance. The younger children experience a gradual transition from the greater community in the yard via an extended ramp with steps to the buildings in which their classrooms are housed. Outside the

Lucien Kroll. Students' halls of residence for the medical faculty of the University of Leuven, Brussels, 1970–71

rooms on the parapet of the gallery are mini-huts, each for two children, from which they can look down on the yard from their safe retreat from a group with which they nevertheless remain in touch. Here at last we see Adolf Behne's remark about the play character of community-orientated rational architecture becoming feasible reality.

Yoshizaka made another important discovery about the formation of groups: in order to be able to achieve spatial determination and to develop, a group needs relative isolation, definition or at least indication of its territory. For this reason he put fragments of wall in front of each classroom in the Kasei school, and in the town planning context he introduced bands of green as boundaries.

Takamasa Yoshizaka and U-Ken. Kaisei School, Nagasaki. 1958

Ralph Erskine's estate designs should also be mentioned here, particularly Bykers's Wall, where a gigantic wall containing dwellings was built around the redevelopment area as a protective rampart against the wide arterial road upon which it stands. Thus the old location retains its identity, and its peace and quiet.

Team Zoo's designs always contain both a hard edge as a boundary, which gives the group security, and a semi-open group form with transitional stages from inside to outside.

From art and symbol to everyday monuments

Takasama Yoshizaka has spoken emphatically about the importance of things for no specific purpose, about art as an essential element of a humane environment. "Efficiency, hitherto very useful, can invade a human being to the extent that he begins to lose himself." In an article written in 1967 entitled "For the liberation of mankind" he asserted that beauty achieved in works of art or architecture, or parts of it, becomes significant as a work of art itself, with the result that works of art are a driving force in the development of a culture.

"Art connects us directly with movements around us, and through the power of imagination it gives shape to inner experiences, which are usually impossible to grasp, and thus it helps us to understand our condition. Although it may seem to be a waste from the point of view of pure efficiency, we need some support in an endlessly extending world made up of parts relating to each other; we should like a symbol of the fact that we are alive, a symbol that says: "I exist in this world." We should build a place which, although it may stand alone, resists standardization and levelling down.

"Why not pay out a great deal of money for a graffiti tower? We must build something from which there is not a pennyworth of profit to be had, something that proclaims our existence."[9]

Team Zoo's buildings, most markedly in the case of the Atelier Mobile, are already crammed with such things to an almost indecent extent; images and symbols lie in wait and surprise us on every corner. Plants and animals show a superfluity of shapes and colours that we, a less decorative creature, would like to create as our expressed self, in contrast with things that are to the point and merely necessary, things that we are compelled to do all the time.

The biologist Adolf Portmann never tired of pointing out that the living world shows a multiplicity of forms that cannot be explained by any possible need for the preservation of species. But that is a characteristic of life, of plasmatic substance, the unmistakable stamp borne by the shape of a species, a stamp that can show excess. Portmann calls this the form of selfrepresentation. It is the form that is there simply for its own sake and thus represents the essence of the self.[10] One should in the same way retain the right of "proclaiming one's existence" by surrounding oneself with an excess of non-functional but beautiful objects.

Yoshizaka always uses elements of excess in his buildings, which give them their individual form, but they are always associated with a particular meaning. He decorates important parts of a building. The upper storey of the Kasei school is sculpted like the head of a proud animal, with heavily protruding ledges and a composition of window frames like a crown set with jewels. This storey contains staff room and offices. In the same way, in the Athené Française the entrance floor with offices has an impressive façade relief between the simple, reiterated concrete frames of the classrooms.

Decoration and symbols are additional playful images, like the eye that looks down at people arriving from the main building in

Inter University Seminar House. Main building

the Seminar Village, or shapes affirming relationship with the cosmos, and emphasis placed on everyday necessities.

The roof of the aeronautical museum near Nara symbolically creates the connection between heaven and earth with a stone staircase to the sky reminiscent of Indian observatory buildings; but it pierces the roof as though a heavenly body had dug its way through a soft hill while crossing the Earth's orbit. This enormous sculpture also collects rainwater from the great roof in the pool in front of it, thus creating a real relationship with the heavens, including a double meaning like the omega-shaped gargoyle on Le Corbusier's chapel at Ronchamp.

The Yoshizaka team has designed many symbolic forms for necessary water or energy-supply plants with friendly technologies. They are intended to represent a new ecological awareness, but also to become great community works as symbols of the new, non-exploitatory relationship with the environment. They are intended to make their mark on the silhouette of the town or village as church towers did in the past.

Takamasa Yoshizaka and U-Ken. Aeronautical Museum, Ikomayama. 1969

A facility of this kind was planned for rebuilding the island of Oshima, which had been destroyed by a volcanic eruption. These were large stone mounds for water collection. Rainwater was intended to flow over the surface of the mound into extensive pools, and inside the mounds water was to precipitate in caves by condensation. The mounds and the huge pools of water would be built by the community themselves. The beautiful shape of the mounds, reminiscent of gigantic Stone Age tombs, and the decorative shapes of the pools were intended to become symbols of the new community and places of religious worship for the island.

This project was never built, but the Yoshizaka team and Team Zoo have designed all kinds of friendly environmental equipment: windmills, shady areas and plants on buildings.

There are examples of such things all over the world, but few have achieved the status of art. At the Rudolf Steiner Seminar in Järna, Sweden, the waste-water cascades are lavishly planted, and are the most beautiful external areas in terms of design. Dirty water from lavatories and wash-basins pulses rhythmically over the bowls, harmoniously shaped to create a wave movement, in order to be enriched with oxygen. Art and the necessities of life are combined.

Buildings by Takasama Yoshizaka and Team Zoo are full of signs, images and literary gestures intended to express new social connections, beyond the programmatic forms of a univer-

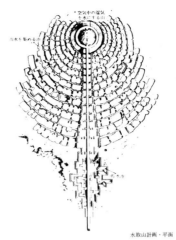

水取山計画・平面

Takamasa Yoshizaka and staff at Waseda University. Rebuilding on Oshima island. Water supply hill. 1966

sity society. In the cement floor at the entrance of the Uratei house is inscribed: "Knock and it shall be opened"; the writing is surrounded by engraved vines.

Creating a world with fewer social constraints is the unbroken thread in the work of Yoshizaka, and it is an optimistic force running through Team Zoo's humorous and playful images. It is the creation of a world in which the atmosphere of freedom, of human ability to create a world beyond immediate purpose, can be fully developed.

Rudolf Steiner Seminar Järna. Sweden. Water purification plant

Epilogue

The elements conquer architecture

The playful force that leads to integration admits everything at first, does not reject anything out of hand. This was the meaning of "Discontinuous Unity". Yoshizaka wrote the following verse:

D	okodemo	Everywhere
I	tsudemo	Always
S	orezorega	Each in his own way
C	onna koto demo	Even something like that
O	moikitte	Courageous
N	andemo	Whatever happens
T	eian shiyō	Let's suggest it!

This means neither lack of consideration nor adaptation with reference to the environment, but characterful interventions arising from different individual views.

For Atelier Iruka architecture is social responsibility; this includes drawing attention to values available on site, to the extent that they represent independence and individual character. Fitting in between what already exists does not necessarily imply restriction. Atelier Zō is always on the look-out for new spatial images, scenes of three-dimensional experience, as if on an endless adventure journey.

Both groups have rediscovered traditional craft techniques for their surfaces – clay and plaster rendering – and unearthed new sources of beauty. For the Atelier Mobile's play with shapes and images becomes play with the building.

Yoshizaka's plan for "Tokyo in the year 2001" provided for articulation of the endless area of buildings by using green zones like the canals of Venice to provide a strong outline for districts of the city and preserve their identity by means of boundaries. Atelier Zō's contribution to the competition "A style for the year 2001"[11], 1985, was called "Accumulation 2001". Articulation by means of buildings and rooms is veiled under all-embracing vegetation, but a thousand niches, holes and spaces in between provide hiding-places and shelter for every kind of living creature. In between them are traces of order, shape and form. It is rather like being an explorer in one of the magnificent Maya cities that had been absorbed by the jungle. Amidst this architecture is open space placed in front of rampant nature – as in gardens by Louis Le Roy, a place of refuge, essential to life and providing order.

Is that fatalism or strategy? At the very least it supersedes the classical notion of architecture as a search for the style of a period, or for styles. The motto remains Paul Scheerbart's playful rhyme about playing games:

"Im Stil ist das Spiel das Ziel.
Im Spiel ist das Ziel der Stil.
Am Ziel ist das Spiel der Stil."[12]

(In style the game is the goal.
In the game the goal is style.
At the goal the game is style.)

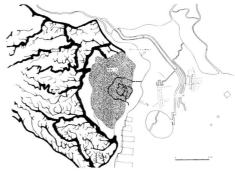

Yoshizaka group. Tokyo in the year 2001. 1970

Notes

1 *The Japan Architect,* December 1956
2 *Le Corbusier,* 1910–1965, Zürich 1986
3 Manfred Speidel, 'Gestaltete Natur. Überlegungen zur japanischen Gartenkunst der Heian-Zeit', in: Jörg Zimmermann (ed.), *Das Naturbild des Menschen,* Munich 1982
4 See p. 32/33
5 Adolf Behne, 'Der moderne Zweckbau', *Bauweltfundamente 10,* Frankfurt/Berlin 1964
6 Manfred Speidel, loc. cit.
7 Le Corbusier, *Kommende Baukunst,* Stuttgart 1926
8 Victor Turner, *Drama, Fields and Metaphors,* Cornell University 1974
9 *Shinkenchiku,* December 1967
10 Adolf Portmann, *Die Tiergestalt,* Freiburg 1965
11 *Shinkenchiku,* 'A Style for the Year 2001', special issue, July 1985
12 *Die Briefe der Gläsernen Kette,* I. B. Whyte and R. Schneider (ed.), Berlin 1986

WILD AND UNCERTAIN TIMES: TEAM ZOO'S SAVOIR-FAIRE

Patrice Goulet

I

You open a Japanese magazine and turn the glossy pages. Everything is clear, neat, impeccable. You look at the photographs: they are are taken straight on, the verticals are parallel, the shadows precise; nothing anecdotal creeps in to distract your attention. You examine the architecture. Volumes are skilfully calculated, articulations correct, openings magnificent, materials gleaming. No objects or human beings turn up to disturb the peace.[1]

You think of Utamaro Ryogoku and Katsushika Hokusai, of Katsura and Ryoanji, of Kenji Mizoguchi and Akira Kurosawa, of Nikon and Sony; you are in an ideal Japan. You have come across nothing in these pages that does not conform with this aesthetic.[2]

You are in Tokyo, walking through the town. Your head is spinning, anxiety seizes you, despair sets in: everything is heterogeneous, chaotic, bogus. Pictures move, underground trains speak, there are telephones in the street, cables in the sky, merchandise on the pavements and the buildings, buildings you saw in the impeccable photographs, are covered with advertising. Consumerism has invaded everything and Kyoto looks like Wuppertal![3]

Then you remember a splendid and terrible book by photographer Shuji Yamada, with leaden skies covering a world in rags, and no man's land of the kind Wim Wenders is so fond of. Total realism. You haven't even seen life boiling and bubbling. You are hypnotized by the defeat of form.[4]

You go to the cinema. You see "Blade Runner" by Ridley Scott: you are living in tomorrow's San Francisco and confirm that it is an extrapolation of today's Tokyo. You see the streets, and see how lively they are. You see buildings and their permeability. You look at the buildings more closely; lines are broken, volumes have been eroded, boundaries have become porous. A multitude of objects and screens are clogging things up. And you think of architects' dreams that believed rigour to be the essence of modernity, you remember Le Corbusier and his negative judgements on the suburbs and New York, his radial, functional and rational town projects and you are aware of the degree of his failure.

You are perplexed. What has happened? What is the meaning of this rejection of order and the rise of the inextricable? What future can there be for architects?

And you pick up the cool magazines again and read about despair and desperate resistance by those who are still dreaming of clarity and limpidity, inexorably driven to produce only works that are certainly pure, minimalist and strong, but at the same time opaque, compact and solitary.

You admire their perseverance and their sacrifice, their demands and their concern about perfection, but you wonder at the same time about the validity and effectiveness of their struggle; putting a rock in the middle of a current only serves to confirm its

strength, installing a paddle wheel would drive a mill. This image produces the question: could architecture exist today that, like the wheel, draws its strength from the energy that is making our towns explode?

And then you recall some rather different and disturbing pages that you passed over rather casually, and go off in search of a very strange article. It is in the October 1981 issue of Kenchiku Bunka and "narrates" the "Shinshukan", a civic centre built by Atelier Zō, the founder group of Team Zoo, in Miyashiro-cho, a community on the outskirts of Tokyo.

Shinshukan Community Center, Miyashiro-cho

It is not a description in the form of a clinical report but a veritable montage, linking, telescoping and superimposing over 60 full pages, panoramic views, tracking shots, zooms, flashbacks, details, sketches and plans as if taken from a film, thus making it clear that this is only a reflection of a story, of a movement.

Some of these pictures are extremely sensual, for example the plan of the curves of a piece of furniture with a texture that irresistibly evokes that of the skin, sometimes they are totally abstract, like the scarcely perceptible strokes (in fact fragments of a design for joinery) written on a concrete partition and looking like trajectories of elementary particles tracked in a bubble chamber, or again a fine, complex and delicate master tracing of a building reproduced on a very indistinct photograph of the surroundings (a field on the horizon, a solitary crowd of little houses placed side by side under immense electricity pylons), which makes one think of an astronomical map.

The message is clear: no image is closed; they always relate to others and within this analogous world forms ceaselessly metamorphose; architecture is shown not like an object but like a living milieu.

Before closing this magazine you realized why you found these pages so strange; it is that they revealed not only architecture in the most elevated sense of the term (that is to say having mastered knowledge and culture) but also that this architecture transcends the wild and dynamic chaos into which it was plunged. What intelligence, sensitivity and humanity did this require from its creators!

II

– What do you mean by humanity? you ask me, astonished, as it is not customary today to talk about notions of this kind in the context of architecture!

– Let us say that it is the quality that makes architecture agreeable to people.

– Agreeable, you say again, what a peculiar word!

– It is so unusual that its absence shows what is lacking in architecture today. We could have written "benevolent" (humanity: a feeling of benevolence towards one's neighbours, says the dictionary), "warm" (showing warmth, animation, life; literally, which warms up) or again "attentive" (showing kindness, attention).

– All this is very sentimental, you will insist. Let us rather establish what you are basing yourself upon when you assert that Team Zoo's architecture is "humanist".

– Clearly on the fact that its ultimate aim seems to be "the human being and his blossoming".

– That's the dictionary definition!

– Let us add then that this blossoming can only take place in open and sensitive surroundings.

– And Zoo's architecture is open?

– Certainly. Firstly (this could be seen in the publication on the Shinshukan) because it presents itself as a milieu and not as an object. Then, because it does not attempt to deny the fact that it is shaped under the impact of particular requirements (of setting, of people) which have modelled it, as it were (this is what makes each of their built projects so different) and that it accepts transformation and ageing, and what is more, encourages it (for example, by being ready to hide itself away under luxuriant vegetation).

Then again, because it shows a complete absence of preconceived ideas, of a priori, of prejudices, a total lack of partisan spirit, a rejection of systems, dogmas, canons that would claim to be the only ones capable of producing good architecture. Finally because it is plural and multi-dimensional and invites a multitude of interpretations.

Town hall, Nago-City, Okinawa

– You said that it was sensitive?

– Meaning that it paid attention, and that beyond functional, structural and aesthetic problems it was essentially preoccupied with satisfying desires expressed by the residents, respecting their customs as well as their feelings.

– For example?

– By ordering from local workers the 56 lions (they are called "shishi", and are the animals that traditionally protect the island) that Zoo placed on the façade of the town hall in Nago, facing the sea (the opposite façade is made up of stepped terraces covered with pergolas, called "asagi", which are also a feature of the region). By making the balustrades at the school in Miyashiro-cho into abacuses. By transforming the children's clinic in Kazura into an elephant.

Children's Clinic, Kazura

In a certain way Zoo is thus following a process similar to that of a resident who personalizes his house by introducing his own fantasies, memories and dreams; this will to remain rooted in this popular world that architects usually have such difficulty in apprehending is certainly one of the secrets of their success.

It is true that like Lucien Kroll, another exception, Zoo does not find banality in this world, but on the contrary a richness that has to be helped to reveal itself and blossom. This attitude is opposed to the Messianic vision that has been such a strong feature of modernity, and is, inversely, very close to the trade of the architect as it was traditionally understood when it was a matter of clinging on to the reality of "others" by bringing them knowledge acquired by reflection and experience.

This explains why their buildings can appear so normal to some, so traditional or even, sometimes, so vulgar to others.

The Kaminokawa showroom built by Atelier Mobile is surely a pretty improbable mixture of undulating roof, a semi-high-tech structure resting on capitals in the shape of birds? The Wakaba nursery school at Hanamaki by the same Atelier Mobile surely has the same silhouette as innumerable buildings that cover Japan today? To say nothing of the houses full of fantasy that architects so detest.

But this first impression never lasts, because all the projects have an indefinable quality which immediately removes them from the realms of the ordinary. And this displacement, one very quickly realizes, is due to a particularly intelligent inventive, original and demanding brand of skill.

The quality and care given to the choice of materials and their application are key factors here. It is thus possible to understand why Zoo has always sought both collaboration with local craftsmen and development of the most modern techniques. (For example, the laser for perfect cutting of their furniture.)

By optimizing traditional methods and transforming new materials they have extraordinarily enlarged the range of tactile and visual sensations that architecture can provide: from exposed and cast concrete in the Shinshukan to the sequences of coloured breeze blocks in Nago town hall, via those at the Nakijin community centre painted a startling red, the angular stones of the long twisting walls of the Okinawa park, with interior masonry covered with faience to the smooth and transparent surfaces of the great hall in Asacho, from woodwork that develops like a musical accompaniment to the punctuation provided by squares of shining ceramic tiles which, for example, link the floor of the gallery and the turfed area of the inner square in the Shinshukan.[5]

Ishikawa Municipal Park, Shirahamahara, Okinawa

Certainly the invention, tactility and intimacy that characterizes Team Zoo's work are reminiscent of Wright and Gaudí. But it is these very additional features that are both worrying and revealing. It is evident in the furniture, which succeeds in making two universes melt into one, thus achieving a veritable squaring of the circle. It is also visible in the Shinshukan in the astonishing complicity between the envelope which, slowly, bends to produce an animal shape which makes one think of Antoni Gaudí and Rudolf Steiner (nothing here more magical than the simplicity of the rising movement of the roof which makes the arches of the courtyard portico melt from a semi-circle to an ellipse) and the repetitive, rhythmic and displaced chains which make these spaces more musical, evoking, this time, Frank Lloyd Wright or Charles Rennie Mackintosh.

It is no doubt another essential key to the success of Team Zoo that they have this capacity to handle heterogeneous things, to reunite, to reconcile, to make extremes collaborate.

Surely this is also the meaning of the flying elephant, a crazy and magnificent notion, that Atelier Zō has taken as its signature and trade mark.

They are constantly concerned to forge links between order and disorder, regularity and irregularity, straight and curved, unique and multiple, symmetry and asymmetry, large and small, smooth and rough, soft and hard, light and dark, opaque and transparent, rustic and refined, traditional and modern, mineral and vegetable, natural and artificial, spontaneous and premedi-tated, anecdotal and essential, everyday and cosmic, thus running counter to all architectural theory that is in constant pursuit of unity, and opposing even more blatantly the processes of purification that have characterized modern functionalist and rationalist architecture.

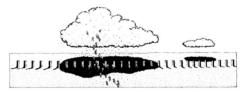

Conceptual sketch of Nakijin Community Center

In Nakijin the purity and abstraction of a hypostyle hall with bright red columns is juxtaposed with an envelope roof, as protective as a turtle's carapace. But this alliance between two archetypes (let us say the labyrinth and the hut) is revealed by its vegetable covering as being in the service of yet a third thing the symbiosis of culture and nature.

In the Shinshukan all geometrical systems collaborate and are transformed as a result of their reciprocal impact. Radiating, concentric, square webs are superimposed and overlap. At the same time, every limit is distorted: the great straight façade, as if under the pressure of exterior space, thus creating a tapered and stretched transitional space, and the two side façades look as if they have been blown up by the interior space.

In Asacho, the typically baroque treatment of the dome is superimposed on references to traditional Japanese architecture. The triangular openings and the precipitous nature of the interior of the cupola are reminiscent of solutions devised by Guarino Guarini for the chapel of the Turin shroud, built on the cathedral apse.

III

Some years ago all these particular features would have been sufficient to put Team Zoo's architecture out of court.

And even today, the way in which they work, the notions they rely on, the objectives they pursue, the buildings that they build are always different from the majority of architects' work in Japan and elsewhere.

Their taste for life, their absolute lack of respect for rules, the pleasure they take in the most active and popular parts of the town, their affection for craftsmen, their enthusiasm for team work, their limitless commitment when elaborating and building each of their projects, their respect for tradition, their will to create places suitable for exalting life rather than immortalizing their own genius, their refusal to be confined within the little world of architecture, the extent of their curiosity, their humour and gaiety all serve to reinforce their "eccentricity".

Worse still, are these "particular signs" not characteristics of that romantic current that the orthodox modern movement so detests and marginalizes? In truth they are, but surely that is more of a positive quality nowadays? The realist doctrine that has so far made the running has succeeded, in other words it has eliminated everything so thoroughly that it has created a vacuum and left us in a state of complete absurdity.

Would it then not be normal for us to look more openly at those people who have maintained their course towards another future, and should we not reconsider the said romantic tendency?

Was it in fact not the only one to appreciate what the rise of science and technology meant for our times by making the "law of change" a fundamental element in architecture?[6]

Was it not the only one to understand the importance of change in a world where knowledge was expanding more and more rapidly?

On these two points, it is clear today that the Modern movement has made a fatal error of interpretation. All the writings on it are based on an apparently unshakeable duality between old and new, as if it was only a shift of emphasis, and that all one had to do was to be on the right side! And surely this error explains the Post-modern reaction, which concluded from the failure of the Ville Radieuse that the solution was to return to things tried and tested. The problem is that it was not a shift, but an acceleration.

This Manichaean vision strengthened the idea that a new order had to be founded. In fact the contrary was true, as this acceleration had to be countered by a search for the greatest faculty for adaptation and artistic creativity. Our towns have paid dearly for this lack of understanding. Their present state shows what happens when forces of this kind are not taken into account. Every attempt to restore a durable new order has failed because every project, however important, has immediately been swallowed up by chaos, finally just making everything all the more brutal.

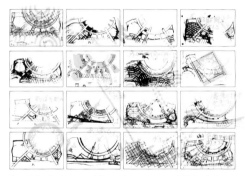

Spatial relations and formal concepts of Shinshukan at Miyashiro-cho

We have certainly a lot to learn today from the kind of architecture that is called wild and that architects so despise. However much one appreciates its forms, one has to note that it has turned out to be much more adaptable, more able to react to fluid situations, more flexible in taking advantage of the slightest opportunity. It has even often succeeded in repairing fabric torn by the effects of architectural doctrines. In this respect Tokyo is a particularly revealing city as so much of this wild element is present, and seems intimately linked with its vitality.

It is not necessary to look far or for long to note how much, in all fields, one is involved today in a revaluation of complex systems, which show both a better image of the fundamental nature of matter (for example the progress of quantum mechanics) and a better operational model for our society.

Hotel in Ifu, Okinawa

Thus one can understand why Team Zoo, beyond its own qualities of warmth and humanity, is part of the avant-garde which, after the disasters of tabula rasa, zoning and segregation, prefers to work with subtlety rather than brutality, practises judo rather than boxing, is concerned to include rather than to separate, strives to manage unstable states rather than to impose artificial order.

This is what constitutes the common denominator of work by architects as diverse as, for example, Lucien Kroll and Coop Himmelblau, Foster and Gehry, Site and Pesce, Nouvel and Koolhaas, Fuksas and . . . Team Zoo, whose complexity strives to respond to the challenge thrown out by the "wild and uncertain times" into which we have plunged in spite of ourselves.

Notes

1 "Architecture is the wise, correct and magnificent play of volumes assembled under light." Le Corbusier

2 Why Utamaro Ryogoku? As a reminder of this "firework" taken to the USA by Frank Lloyd Wright in 1916.

3 Wuppertal because of Wim Wender's film "Alice in den Städten".

4 Nihon Mura: *Ten years of photographs by Shuji Yamada, 1969–1979*. The majority of the photographs of the Shinshukan published in *Kenchiku Bunka* are by S. Yamada.

5 Their disposition is reminiscent of the Tofuku-Ji garden in Kyoto.

6 "The order of change is limitless and profound. I have searched for its nature. I have tried to see it as a principle. For a long time I saw it as a reality. It is perhaps, as Heraclitus said, the only reality we see." Frank Lloyd Wright, *An Autobiography*. New York 1977.

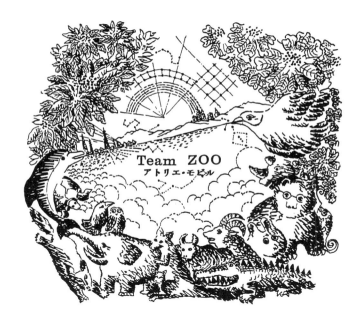

THE MEMBERS OF TEAM ZOO

Team Zō (Elephant) was founded in 1971 by a group of colleagues from U-Ken, Professor Takamasa Yoshizaka's architectural office, and members of his urban development staff at Waseda University. One reason behind this move was commissions for cities on the Okinawa Islands, which had been returned to Japan.

Atelier Mobile (Running Bird) was founded by Kinya Maruyama at the same time.

From 1979 membership of Team Zō increased, Tsutomu Shigemura was appointed to the University of Kobe, Hajime Sakugawa returned to Okinawa, and different focal points emerged for work in urban and regional planning. All these factors led to reorganization in several groups, independent from each other but co-operating on various projects; the groups adopted names, almost all animals, in order to show their spiritual and intellectual interrelationship in a humorous fashion, and called themselves 'Atelier'.

A play on words led to a change from the original Team Zō (Elephant) to Team Zoo.

The animal names are illustrated with animal pictures, used as atelier trade marks. A graphic design shows the development of the groups.

In the following pages projects are presented with Team Zō's first, as the core group, followed by the work of the various ateliers.

Team Zō (Elephant) 1971–1978

Founder members 1971

Keiko Arimura	Iruka
Hiroyasu Higuchi	Zō
Koichi Otake (died 1983)	Zō
Tsutomu Shigemura	Iruka
Reiko Tomida	Zō

Members until 1978

Kenichiro Kikuno	1971–82	Kuma
Munenori Kanazawa	1971–72	
Masamitsu Yoshizaka	1971–78	
Tami Kondo	1972–74	
Hidekazu Hirai	1975–80	Wani
Hajime Sakugawa	1975–78	Gaii
Sadaomi Nishio	1975–82	Shura
Kasuyuki Tamura	1975–76	
Miwako Kikuchi	1975–80	Kuma
Akira Ono	1977–82	Todo
Taeko Nagayama	1977–82	
Masasumi Matsui	1977–82	Todo

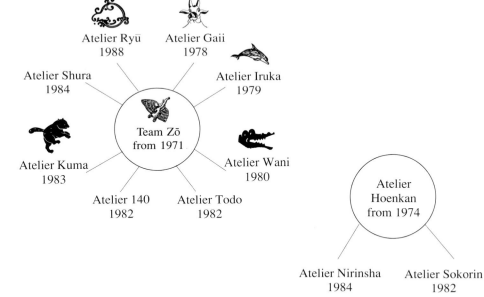

Other cooperating ateliers

Atelier Baku	presentation and drawings
Paper Studio	graphic design
Shuji Yamada	ceramics and photography

Atelier Mobile (Running Bird)
from 1969; architecture and furniture
Kinya Maruyama
Yasuo Okada
Toshihide Tsutsui
Tsutomu Itoh
Douglas Ross
Naotaka Arima

Atelier Hoenkan (Square-Circle Building)
from 1974; furniture and timber interiors
Kazumasa Sakamoto
Keiji Shiina
Taro Hosokawa

Atelier Gaii (Bull)
from 1978; architecture
Hajime Sakugawa (previously Team Zō)

Atelier Iruka (Dolphin)
from 1979; architecture
Tsutomu Shigemura (previously Team Zō)
Keiko Arimura (previously Team Zō)
Masao Yoshimura
Keiko Yagi
Motoyuki Majima
Hayato Kubo
Stan Russel
Hiroyuki Ueda
Joan Goncha (since 1990)
Aya Okayama (since 1990)
left between 1988 and 1990:
Tomoko Nakagawa
Rumi Nozaki
Shiro Mukai (founded Atelier 101)
Takako Kudo
Hideo Nishiyama
Junichi Yoshida
Hideki Goto
Emi Sakamoto
Kensu Zaima (now Atelier Mobile)

Atelier Zō (Elephant)
from 1979; architecture and town planning
Hiroyasu Higuchi
Reiko Tomita
Fumio Uchida
Ichiro Machiyama
Shoichi Ikeda
Toru Ohta
Hajime Uehara
Takaaki Satoh

Shigeru Sakamoto
Eirai Iwata
Tamegoro Nagata
Ikuyo Seki
Masako Nunokawa
Satoshi Tanada

Atelier Wani (Crocodile)
from 1980; regional planning
Hidekazu Hirai (previously Team Zō)

Atelier Sokorin (Original-Craft-Wood)
from 1982; furniture and timber interiors
Keizo Hatto (previously Hoenkan)

Atelier Todo (Sea Lion)
from 1982; architecture
Akira Ono (previously Team Zō)
Masasumi Matsui (previously Team Zō)

Atelier 140
from 1982
Atsushi Ishimaru (previously Atelier Zō)

Atelier Kuma (Bear)
from 1983; architecture and
regional planning
Kenichiro Kikuno (previously Team Zō)
Setsuko Abe (previously Atelier Zō)
Miwako Kikuchi (previously Team Zō)
Hiroaki Ishida
Yoko Yamada

Atelier Shura
from 1984; architecture
Sadaomi Nishio (previously Team Zō)
Hiroshi Hibino
Mitsuo Mizuno
Miki Asai

Atelier Nirinsha (Two-Wheeler)
from 1984; timber work
Kazuo Sekiya (previously Hoenkan)

Atelier Kujira (Whale)
from 1986; architecture
Akiyoshi Okamura (previously Atelier Mobile)

Atelier Ryū (Dragon)
from 1988;
Fumio Uchida (previously Atelier Zō)
Yasuo Okada (previously Atelier Mobile)

ALPHABET

"What we are thinking of . . ." was Team Zō's contribution to the exhibition "A New Wave of Japanese Architecture", which visited ten cities in the USA in autumn 1978. It presented work by the founder members, before the group broke up to form several ateliers. Pictures were linked associatively with concepts in alphabetical order.

Dignity	Mountain mimicry	Sky sea sun science
Earth covered with numerous cracks	form should not seek after Novelty	Tombstone
Feminine and masculine	Order – we are searching for	Universe is packed in architecture
Joy jail	Pray play	Vast vernacular void
Kaleidoscope	Quadrillion	Wind
Light and shadow organize architecture	Red repetition	Xerography xylograph

Komaki city library

1F. plan   2F. plan   3F. plan   section

museum for children in kinder land   Komaki city library   domo celakanto

Yoga
Zodiac zigzag zoetrope zombie **Z**oo

TEAM **ZOO**

DOMO SERAKANTO

Kamakura, Kanagawa Prefecture, 1974

Going up through a thicket of assorted trees in Kamakura, one can see the ocean in three directions. The long fan shaped site is on a steep slope which goes down towards the west from the road on the top.

It took the owner two years to find this place. They took us to the site in the summer of 1972. What came out from almost three years of struggle was a coelacanth that crawled out from ancient sea.

Domo Serakanto, with its gills, spine, horn, cilium, teeth, antennae and scales appeared in the wind and sank in the light.

Domo Serakanto is a fish dreaming about architecture, an architecture dreaming about fish.

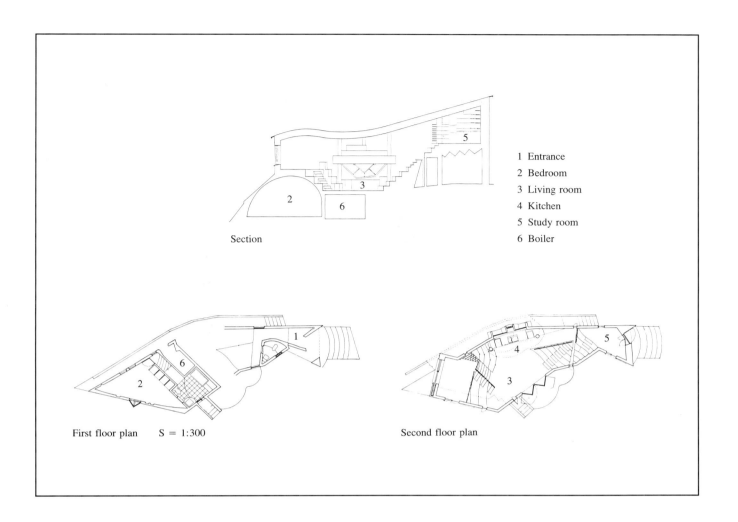

Section

1 Entrance
2 Bedroom
3 Living room
4 Kitchen
5 Study room
6 Boiler

First floor plan   S = 1:300

Second floor plan

Kitchen window

Bedroom

The living rooms is a ravine

DOMO ARABESKA

Tokyo, 1974

Turned off from Ome Avenue. A neighbourhood where outworn and remodeled houses stand right by each other. Domo Arabeska is also a residence that was worn by 50 years of time, and was born again. Land does not change, and neither do people that live there. Tools, pillars, beams, chairs, tables, windows, shoji and even tiles have become familiar. The house is trying to come alive. These things are set like a mosaic, and the blood that has been flowing since the old time keeps on flowing continuously. That's how I want the house to be. Domo Serakanto was a fish that melted into the water. Domo Arabeska is a flower that has become a stone. Bow window of the living room that was at the dark corner on north side of the torn-down house is now set in a place where there is sun. Bow window that had to listen to a faltering sound of a piano for decades.

1 Entrance

2 Kitchen

3 Dining room

4 Living room

5 Terrace

6 Tatami room

7 Bathroom

8 Individual room

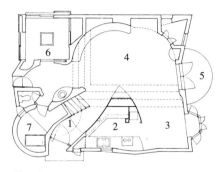

First floor plan   S = 1:250

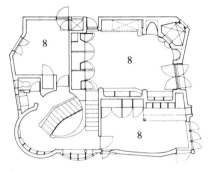

Second floor plan

Expressionistic details,
designed after a trip to Amsterdam

Entrance between plaster leaves

Staircase

Old bow window reused

NAKIJIN COMMUNITY CENTER

Okinawa Prefecture, 1975 (In cooperation with Atelier Mobile)

The community center was positioned as "a construction for all the villagers that can be used freely and readily for a variety of purposes".

The site is on a small plateau of coral (Okinawa limestone) in the center of the village, on the south side of the town hall. The village lies at the foot of Mt. Otowa, in a location full of green vegetation surrounded by eel beds, farms and a cemetery.

A large roof, unique in style and adapted to the particular need, covers the entire enclosure and forms it into a single consolidated structure. This is the first characteristic feature of the planning of space for this community center.

The various rooms are distributed in a huge shady area created by the concrete roof, which is supported by 276 red pillars. Between each room, and between the rooms and the outside, there is a semi-enclosed space equal in area to the indoor space (717 sq. m. of semi-enclosed floor space out of 1,455 sq. m. of construction space), to be utilized for small meetings, workshops, exhibitions and parties.

The second feature is the enclosure of the courtyard with the 276 red pillars. The courtyard which is open on the south side is surrounded on the other three sides by a colonnade formed by the pillars, and the interiors of the rooms which can be seen through the walls, unifying the internal and external space by smoothly connecting the interior and the courtyard. A third feature is that the entire roof is covered with plants: Merremia Tuberosa Rendle (a wooden convulvulus) and bougainvillea. This is not only to increase the insulating effect of the roof, but also to assimilate the building to the surrounding landscape, and to change its expression with the change of seasons. It goes without saying that what we had in mind was the view of red pillars standing out strongly amidst the dark greens.

Local constructional methods, such as wide use of concrete block which is the most popular material in Okinawa for pillars and walls, as well as inlay of seashells on floors and slabs, and local labour, as with the tea house built by the village people, have been preferred everywhere in the building.

Red pillars enveloped in green

Cross section
S = 1:180

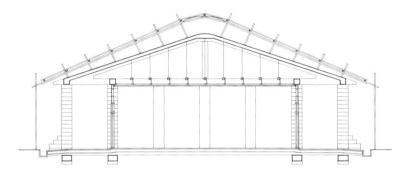

Longitudinal section
S = 1:300

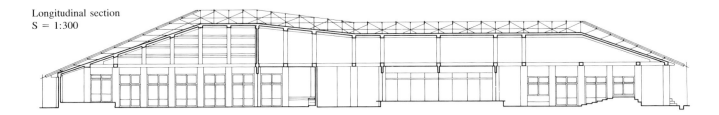

Courtyard

1 Hall with stage
2 Bathroom
3 Audio-visual room
4 Tatami rooms
5 Outside stage
6 Cooking classroom
7 Tea corner
8 Seminar room
9 Library
10 Office and reception room

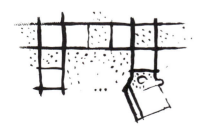

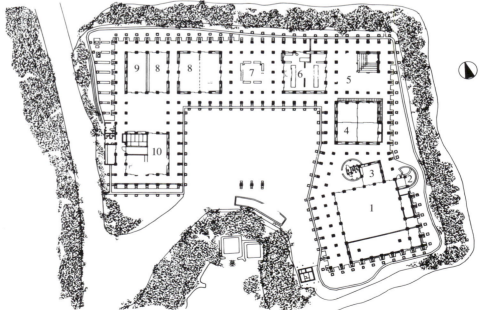

Floor plan   S = 1:800

Outside stage under roof

TEAM ZOO: ATELIER GAII

FUSUI-NO-IE
(HOUSE OF THE WINDS AND WATERS)

Naha, Okinawa Prefecture, 1979

The heat and humidity of the Okinawa summer made protection from the sun and optimal ventilation this residential building's principal requirement. Individual rooms are arranged in two storeys around a hall. Protection from the sun is afforded by shade-producing walls in hollow concrete blocks with wooden-slatted adjustable shutters. The roof is planted with grass for heat insulation purposes. The ceilings of the hall rise diagonally, so that hot air can rise, as in traditional tobacco drying lofts on the islands. A system of channels under the floors and flues in the walls connected with the outside allows the constant wind to be used to ventilate the rooms. A square hole in the hall floor can also be used for seating: the air under the floor circulates around one's legs, a pleasantly cooling experience.

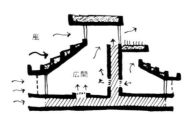

1 Kitchen
2 Dining room
3 Living room
4 Tatami room
5 Car port
6 Sleeping rooms

First floor plan   S = 1:250   Second floor plan

UMI-NO-IE
(SEA HOUSE)

Naha, Okinawa Prefecture, 1984

Ventilation, relationship with the sea and the shape of the rooms combine to form an unusual structure: from outside the house looks organic, like part of a sea creature, but the interior makes absolute sense. The raised floor of the living-hall covers a ventilation cavity, crooked, rising ceilings facilitate the flow of air, and a semi-circular light and air grille above the hall acts as a seat in the stairwell, so that one can enjoy a view of the sea from above.

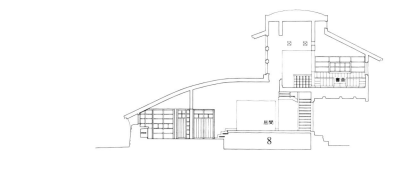

1 Entrance
2 Living room
3 Dining place
4 Kitchen
5 "Sea room"
6 Sleeping room
7 Children's room
8 Wind channel

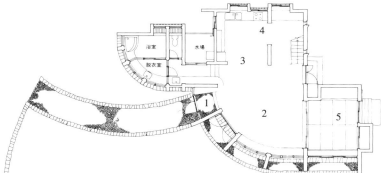

First floor plan   S = 1:250

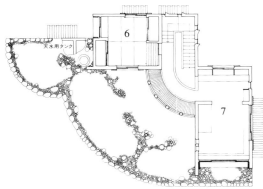

Second floor plan

METHOD OF DISCOVERY OR DISCOVERY OF THE METHODS
– TO RECOVER THE MYTHS –

Concept as a premise

1. What should come after 'Modern'?

"Look, over there live our enemies." A rumour has it that Le Corbusier often said this to his assistants in the roof garden of his atelier, Rue de Savres 35, pointing in the direction of the buildings where the Ecole des Beaux Arts was located. Since then the old enemies of Modern architecture have gradually disappeared. Where do we find our enemies now?

The pioneers of Modern architecture were lucky: they didn't have much to worry about. They believed that science and technology could save human beings and their society, and that there was no ambivalence between technology and its aesthetic on one hand and the values of the age on the other. All were one. Let's take pilotis as an example. This technique seemed to liberate buildings from the restraints of gravity and expressed the absence of bonds with the earth – bonds which had seemed to be symbolic of the limits of human possibilities and as such for all the values of the old society. It was a time when the same aspirations filled the dreams of boys and the lyric expressions of poets. Already in 1910 a young Japanese socialist had voiced this sentiment in a poem which began: "Look, where in that high sky the airplane flies . . ." Such boyish dreams appeared to come true through technology and coincided with the image of the future society.

Of course there are many examples of this liberation. Roof gardens or flat roofs got rid of the heavy roofs which had seemed to symbolize quaint old dignities. Industrial materials and construction methods ensured that architecture reached ordinary people instead of building merely for a few privileged minorities.

The same process took place in Japan except during the ultra-nationalistic period and the Second World War when the 'Teikan-Yoshiki' or Imperial Crown Style flourished, influenced by the atmosphere of the time. It was a mixture of neo-classicism and the traditional style, but in which local influences contributed only a kind of anachronistic dignity and Japanese roofs appeared over multi-storied buildings.

In the sixties the Metabolists made their appearance as the last heirs to an almost religious belief in the supremacy of technology. Infrastructure was compared to the trunk of a tree, minor structures to the branches, and changeable units to the leaves. At first the results seemed to give variety to the monotonous industrialized shape of modern cities, but they ended up as another limitation because they didn't grow as they were supposed to. They were unmasked as just another fashion and the similarity of the units reminded the people of their over-administrated society in which the individuals identity was fading. In fact, variation inside a rigid grid combined with a centrally-controlled system doesn't do anything about the limitations of the totality itself. It is just like a system camera with many optional parts: it's only possible to select the units and not to contribute to the system in a more than indirect way.

But I don't want to be as narrow-minded as to deny acknowledgement of their efforts to escape from the disappointing blind alley in which Modern architecture had brought both Japanese and Westerners. Before, the ground level, which had been cleared thanks to several basement floors and tall buildings, often formed nothing more than a cold white plain where wind and urban crime raged like uncontrollable diseases. Furthermore, industrialization reduced the application of local materials and methods. And airconditioning removed the need for characteristic regional features and made identification sometimes very difficult.

Hospitals are a rather good example: everything from the general layout to the minor details is designed with the latest evolution in medical machinery in mind, but the result is that for patients and visitors hospitals become a colder environment than ever before.

As for other community facilities, most architects are forgetful that these belong to the biggest buildings of a community and that traditionally meetings had been held in a temple, a shrine or the biggest private house, regardless of particular purpose or frequency. Every community member knows that the value of a meeting session is never directly related to its frequency. More often than not it's the other way round. So designers should keep in mind that they have to accommodate the biggest and most important functions in the best way, if it is necessary to establish priorities. Also the building's image must be representative for all members whereas it is actually often based on dated standards or on symbols which do not fit the community. Therefore many so-called culture centers are rejected by parts of the community because they have the wrong impression about them.

The Petroleum Crisis indirectly caused some afterthoughts by the vanguards belonging to the main current of Japanese architecture. They changed their minds about conceptional expressionism or aestheticism, which might be interpreted as a sign of weakness or even defeat when compared to the period when they were only too eager to investigate the real effects of architecture. Today we do not hear such debate anymore but rather introvertive theories, except for a small group of optimists of a new kind among whom I count myself for the simple reason that I still believe that architecture has a very wide role to play.

Why indeed are the unplanned and chaotic cities and villages more fascinating than the coldness and boredom of modern architecture, even though the features of older days are fading away? Maybe because we feel that in those complex fruits of behavioural integration there still exists an environment for

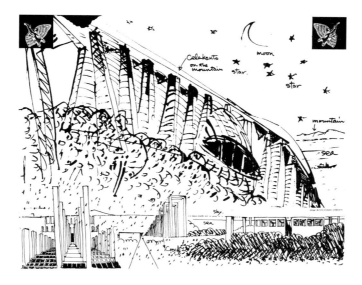

human dramas of contingency and encounter. So why don't we produce the same opportunities in planned architecture?

2. Dis-Cont for discontinuous unity

Takamasa Yoshizaka has been one of the architects who intends to pass the limits of Modern architecture by means of observing human space and the mental process of environment comprehension. He is also known as an explorer and indeed as a mountaineer.

In 1958 he proposed the theory of 'Discontinuous Unity', nicknamed Dis-Cont, as the concept of discipline for architectural planning and design. The following is just a summary.

Discontinuous Unity may exist as well in human society as in human space, like our atmosphere in which the individual constituents retain a separate unity and yet participate in the whole, in our case the context of the human group. Of course this leads to the rule of ideal democracy in which each member's individuality is protected, though the group has its own identity in relation to the human space.

Referred to architecture this means that in a single building all parts like floors, walls and ceilings assert themselves while composing one space and that generally there is a relation between each unit and the whole complex.

This concept can be found clearly expressed in Yoshizaka's projects and his city planning and especially in the 'Daigaku Seminar House', an Inter University Seminar House located in a suburb of Tokyo. It is possible to illustrate his ideas by the site planning, the shape and features of each unit and the treatment of details. Yoshizaka himself states that our psychological background has a range from infinitesimal to infinite, but that when we analyze them to reveal, perceive or recognize them we have to do this by dividing and cutting the existing continuity. But without the application of certain rules this will result in complete chaos. What we want is an order by which to restore the complex unity. Thus these mental processes going on in each mind at any time suggest directly this discontinuous unity, our usual way of cognition.

3. Discovery-like Method

Discontinuous Unity, or Dis-Cont, was the relation which would or should exist between different kinds of architecture or between different architectural elements. Of course it is also necessary to relate architecture or environmental design to its surroundings. That's exactly what our 'Discovery-like method', 'Hakkenteki-hoho', is meant to take care of.

It was presented in 1975 by Yoshizaka's group, including Team Zō and me, and published as the 'Method through Discoveries' in Toshi Jutaku (August 1975). Though consisting of many papers this theory is based on a common recognition and design methodology.

When we design, be it a house or a city, the site is of course not a white paper, so every designer attaches at least some importance to it. But we consider it to be more than a condition or a limitation; we see 'hidden resources' in the site or situation in the sense that most of the answer for the problem or at least the germ of the solution is hidden there.

Not only the bureaucracy but also architects and designers suffer from the tendency to prepare the basics of their answers unconsciously in a very early stage because much of their information stems from their own and other's historical experiences. Even though they try to understand the site and its situation, their unconscious prejudices just happen to be the answer, regardless of their efforts.

Of course I don't deny that we are all inclined to express ourselves to individualism and self-expression, but we do want to play in accord, listening to find out what kind of sounds our partners might be playing. Similarly, in Japanese 'Budo', the philosophy behind the samurai martial arts, there is the notion called 'Munen Muso', which refers to a certain state of passivity free of all ideas and thoughts, like in Zen-Buddhism, and which enables the masters to understand a situation which might continue to be peaceable or develop in an instantaneous fight. Naturally I am not a samurai-fighter, but this Munen Muso state of mind suggests us a lot of things regarding the relation to a surrounding situation.

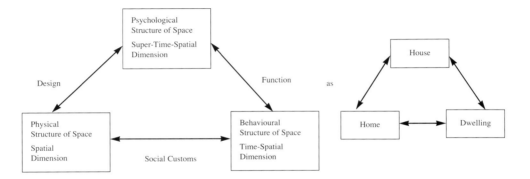

We think that fieldwork is very important to discover something that could be one of the defining elements, comparable to distinguishing something like the sounds of different musicians. Through fieldwork we can discover many things to be included in the future structure of a space. This structure may sometimes be very clear, exist in reality and be plain to view, but sometimes it is to be found in the minds of the people who live near the site. This psychological structure might appear in some modest physical form somewhere or might appear in the behaviour or the customs of the inhabitants. This relation between psychological and physical structure is shown in the figure above.

Whether the designer takes this relation seriously and wishes to develop it, or, on the contrary, makes light of it to create a totally new one, it is important to know about its existence. Otherwise, in the case some structure stays hidden it might manifest itself physically or appear as a kind of reaction. As the permanent character of environmental design and planning gives it a kind of prophetic role, this consideration is very reasonable.

Images from Okinawa islands

If architects were able to conjecture what sort of image his clients keep in mind about a not yet existing building, their work would become easier than that of any other professional.

Local features are another important aspect to be looked for. Of course, in Japan as well as elsewhere, regional characteristics stemming from the feudal age are marked, not only in the country but also in the largest city of the world where we still find the distinctive coloration and features of each district. And though this may be as true for other metropolises in the world, in the sense that even the smallest streetcorner is holding its identity, most of the time we tend to ignore it. Thus it is very important to determine the local characteristics of a place, and sometimes materials, construction methods and the architectural response to climate and other vernacular aspects will play an important role in this determination.

In this context, the problem of participation comes to the forefront, because this determining process is impossible when designers and other decision makers don't speak a common language. If this isn't the case, it's up to the designer to adapt himself.

Many other aspects could be pointed at, all of which should or might be hit upon by this way of field survey which thus becomes

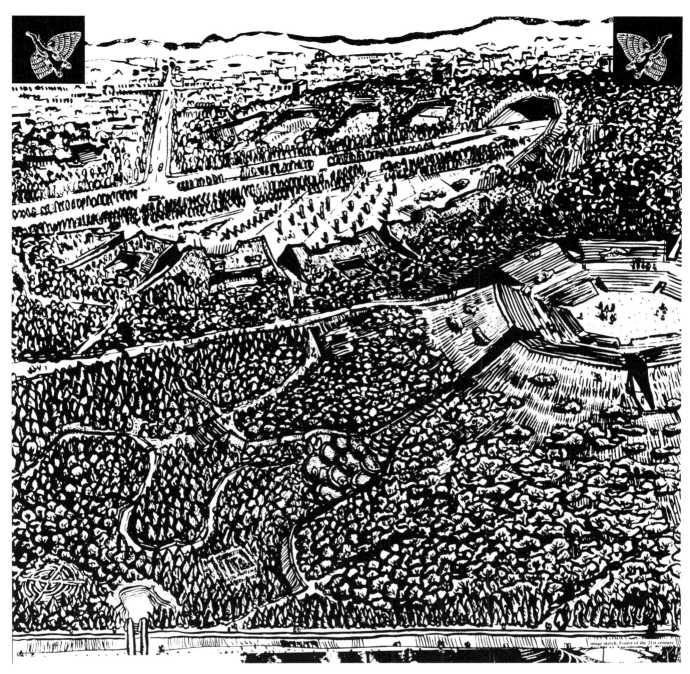

Forest of the 21st century. Reclaimed land; Nago, Okinawa

very interesting and joyful work, comparable to an exploration. For me this fieldwork methodology became a way of life which I enjoy whenever I come into contact with a human environment, even when this isn't necessary in the frame of some design proposal.

Any architecture or environmental design developed through another procedure can be compared to a sea-voyage without charts: even when the destination is sure, the ship's captain must carry them.

Take life itself: it is a lot more interesting when we explore it as a child than when we contemplate it seated at a desk. In modern life, where internationalism and regionalism coexist, where actuality and memory work together, it becomes possible to select both popularized industrial methods and handicrafts for the same purpose. Doesn't this contribute to the fascination felt when we encounter urban contrasts?

Tsutomu Shigemura

This article was part of the contribution of Tsutomu Shigemura to the symposium 'Ecology and Design' in Delft in 1980.

WAKIMACHI LIBRARY

Wakimachi, Tokushima Prefecture, Shikoku, 1986
(In cooperation with Shigemura Seminar, Kobe University)

Can a group of old, earth-walled storehouses be revived and converted to house a new library?

Walking south along the Otani river, beneath a dense canopy of willow boughs, we come to the junction of Nakamichi street, a narrow backroad which meanders off to the east between high, white plaster walls of aged storehouses and townhouses. Continuing along Nakamichi street we catch a glimpse, to the right, through an opening in the wall, of a traditional style ryokan (hotel) with its neatly kept garden. To the left, between its blackstone base and its tile roof, the wall bears large kanji characters in high relief. The wall's tile roof with it's strong horizontal line seems to cover the road like a canopy. After years of neglect, the wall leans away from the street, its plaster is barely clinging in some places while in others it has fallen away completely revealing the wooden lath beneath. In recent years, the row of rustic houses along the narrow streets of Wakimachi have struck the eyes of many admiring sightseers. However, as late as 1984 these valuable cultural assets were being destroyed and replaced by new development, without regard for Wakimachi's cultural heritage.

In 1984 I organized research to study the historical townscape of Wakimachi. As a result of that study, we identified a group of old storehouses and the adjoining wall as the keystone of the town. At the same time a group of Wakimachi citizens recognized the importance of this same storehouse complex and they proposed that it should be restored. One building was to be used as a museum to house the town's traditional festival float. Could this badly deteriorated wall and the adjacent storehouses be saved? Through our design, we hoped to show how new construction and renovation can be combined to revitalize and update the image of an historic townscape.

When we found the site, it consisted of four Dozo-style storehouses, a connected wall, and a newer, two-storey building which formerly housed the offices of the agricultural corporation union. The storehouses and wall wrapped around an intimate inner court which had a well and a small shrine. It was a favorite shortcut through town where friends met by chance and stopped and chatted briefly, before continuing on their ways. Small children played while their parents sat and discussed the topics of the day. These hubs of social interaction, where the built environment facilitates and encourages the informal gathering of people, are critical to the life of small towns and cities alike. We must not allow them to disappear. The old storehouse buildings were constructed in 1872 as the shop and residence of a wealthy kimono dealer. Later in 1921, the farmer's trust union took ownership of the premises and remodeled the buildings. During their remodeling they cut the main beam of the wall and removed its buttresses, leaving it laterally unsupported. When we found the wall in 1984 it was deteriorating and leaning away from the road as a result of long neglect.

In April of 1985, Wakimachi town hall asked me, as the leader of the project H. O. P. E. (housing for proper environment) group, to submit a fundamental design for the new library and a restoration plan for the old storehouses. At that time, I organized a team consisting of the design offices, Atelier Iruka of Kobe city and Takeshi Architects of Tokushima city along with construction expert Canatoni of Kobe University.

The most difficult technical problem that we faced in the design of the new library was how to straighten the old wall and join it to a new structural system. Hiroshi Minotani, a structural dynamics expert from Kobe University, proposed a cantilever system to support the new roof and to give lateral stability to the old wall. It was necessary to cantilever the roof from the colonnade because our new foundations had to be as far as possible from the existing wall so as not to disturb the adjacent soil conditions. The connection between the old wall and the ends of the cantilevered beams was a difficult one where old timber, new steel and reinforced concrete all came together. From the method we developed for structuring the roof of the children's reading room, we generated a fundamental spatial language which we carried through the rest of the design. From the children's library, which fronts the inner court, we wrapped the roof around and surrounded the court with the new library functions. The two existing storehouses, adjacent to the inner court, will be renovated for future use as book and document storage. The two-storey office building of the agricultural corporation union was demolished to make room for the new library.

A narrow promenade stretches from Minamimachi Street back, between the new building and two storehouses, to the inner court. One of the storehouses will be renovated as a museum to house the town's traditional festival float, and the other will become a community lounge. Both are connected to a display gallery which stretches along the old storage wall. More than just a library, this complex of buildings, with its blend of old and new architecture and its diversity of space and function, serves as a community cultural center, with the potential to host a broad spectrum of activities.

How should we design the image of a region where the traditional architecture has been revived and the people have recaptured their sense of place and origin?

In August of this year, Christian Norberg-Schulz of Oslo University gave a lecture at Hokkaido University to the Architectural Institute of Japan. In his lecture, Norberg-Schulz emphasized the importance of 'namable objects' in architecture. If we evaluate the townhouses of Wakimachi city in terms of his theory, we find that they are a veritable treasure chest of such namable objects. The roofs made of the old style with Hongawara tiles, carry symbolic demons which peer at you, as tile animals seem to stroll casually along the ridge. The plaster walls bear Kanji characters in relief while the inside edge of pediments display a variety of plaster motifs. Street level windows have traditional Koshi or privacy screens made of vertical strips of wood, while the upper storey windows are covered with plaster grills in a grid pattern. The Koshi of Wakimachi are composed of particularly thick vertical members which project a very strong and distinct character. At the base of walls, stone is a common foundation and sheathing material. In addition, stone and gravel are used in many places as an earth covering material. Perhaps the most distinctive feature of the Wakimachi townhouses is the Udatsu, a forward extension of the party wall designed to inhibit the spread of fire from one house to the next. The Udatsu, which is capped with Hongawara tiles and a symbolic demon, tapers out at the top like the bow of a ship, emphasizing the horizontal line and giving the row of houses a sense of stability.

With our design for the Wakimachi town library, we wanted to continue the tradition of namable objects, materials, and craftsmen's techniques, which have a deep meaning to the people of the region. Our general design strategy was to be faithful to the traditional forms and materials where our new facade met with the existing historical facades.

On the south elevation of the new building, which is adjacent to the existing facades of Minamimachi Street we attempted to be very sensitive to the composition of the old row-houses. However, around the corner, along the east elevation which fronts the promenade, we gave ourselves more freedom of interpretation in our choice of shapes and materials. The columns along the promenade and wrapping the inner court extend out at the top in a manner which is reminiscent of the Udatsu. The timber sash pattern of the windows along the east elevation of the reading room and surrounding the inner court make reference to the traditional grill patterns without copying the original designs. Within the building, away from the direct influence of the traditional aesthetic, we introduced many new shapes and colors creating a new aesthetic and a collection of namable and memorable spaces.

With our furniture design, we attempted to create a series of objects which would give each space within the library a different and memorable identity. The bookshelf design, based on the form of the row-house, gives the reading room a sense of relationship to the Wakimachi townscape and a special sense of identity. With our chair design, we attempted to emulate human character. The children's chairs have an elementary sense of innocent simplicity, while the larger chairs seem to have grown out of the simpler forms into more developed, adult-like forms. As an example of the creative engagement of artisans the local rooftile maker may be mentioned. He developed several special tile details to fit the particular idiosyncrasies of the roof design. He designed one tile type to fit a concrete roof slab and another to fit the sawtoothed roof to the left of the main entrance. In addition, he designed a special top tile for the parapet wall as well as many symbolic demons and animals.

Our history is formed by transparent layers of time. As long as we can see back through these layers from the present to the past, we retain our sense of culture and origin. When the present and the past coexist history maintains its sense of transparency. However in our modern age, new development without spots for pride or lovable spaces has become dominant. The old environment is fading or has already disappeared. History is losing its sense of transparency and we are losing our sense of origin. According to the functionalist ideal of the modern industrial age, it is wrong to use the same plan for two different functions. According to this ideal, each different type of function must have a particular space designed for that purpose. In our recent past many important buildings have been destroyed because their original function had become obsolete. Just below the surface of our sprawling cityscapes, many important elements of our past remain obscured from view by insensitive neighbours. We must act now to revive the fading namable objects of our environment, as well as create new ones, thus recovering the balance of old and new and maintaining the transparency of time. The original storehouse complex in Wakimachi was a very memorable urban space, surrounded by namable objects. We felt that our design for Wakimachi library should replace the missing and restore the faded namable objects of this important cultural property, thus restoring its function as a vital urban space.

Tsutomu Shigemura

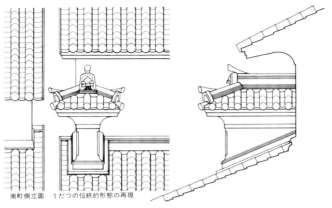

南町側立面　うだつの伝統的形態の再現

Roof of the south side
with traditional details of separating fire wall "Udatsu"

South side of the library in congruence with traditional houses

View into the court

View from the court towards the south with a narrow passage

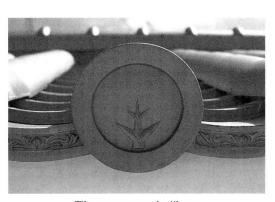

Tile ornaments at the library

Traditional roof ornaments

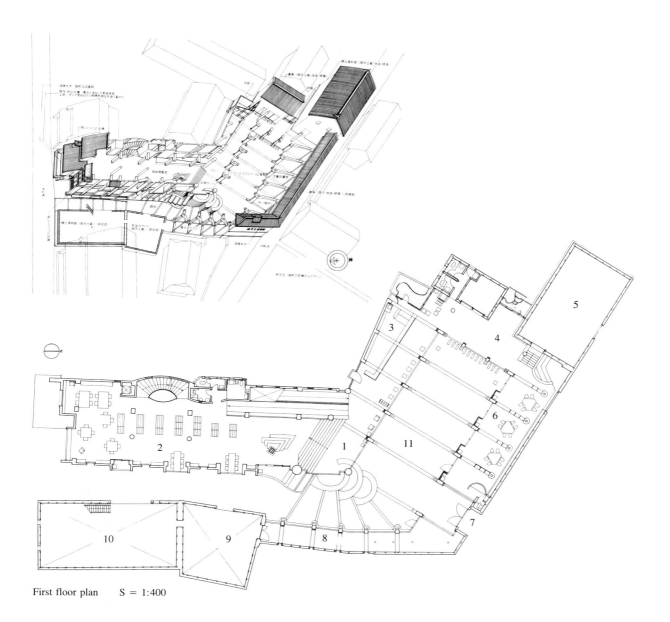

First floor plan   S = 1:400

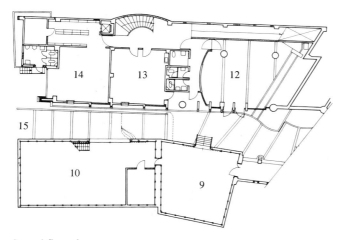

Second floor plan

1 Entrance
2 Library
3 Administration
4 Ethnographic department
5 Ethnographic Archive
6 Children's library
7 Entrance from Nakamachi Street
8 Art gallery
9 Photo Exhibition of old buildings
10 Museum for festival floats
11 Courtyard
12 Meeting room
13 Townscape consultation
14 Garage for library bus
15 Entrance from Minamimachi Street

View of the gallery

Meeting room under the library

Entrance to the library

Children's reading room with the old wall

Art gallery

DOMO CONKULA

Kobe, 1983

In the hilly landscape at the foot of Mount Rokko near Kobe on a site where these hills have been destroyed about 15 years ago to reclaim soil for the artificial Port Island, two kilometres off the Kobe coast, a rather dull housing area of private houses and rental apartments has been built.

In the middle of it in a trapezoid lot of 230 sqm, the 'Spiral Shell', Conkula, has settled and gives the faceless area a distinctive character. The semicircular concrete wall protects the private area from penetrating views. It gives the upper living room a spatial continuum and makes the exterior gentle in character.

View from the entrance hall towards terrace

Entrance hall

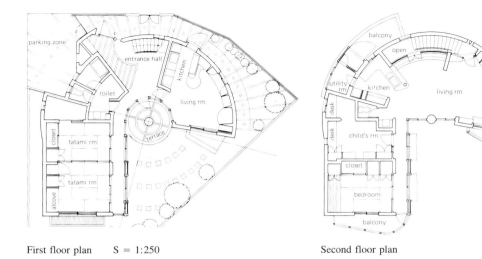

First floor plan   S = 1:250   Second floor plan

DOMO EL TERO
(NISHIDA-TEI)

Shingu-cho, Hyogo Prefecture, 1985

This small family house – the wife is a painter – is in a little village with many well-preserved clay-rendered buildings, about an hour north of the town of Himeji. Clay is still the ideal wall material to provide a comfortable interior climate in hot and humid central Japan. Walls and roof of the house consist of a timber framework, economically reinforced by a visible steel frame. The walls were constructed in the traditional way on a bamboo grid, then clay was applied to a thickness of 8 to 10 cm. The exterior surface is coloured lime rendering with a fresco. The interior lime rendering has a glossy surface in places. This work was skillfully done by Akira Kusumi, Awajishima.

The house is a fine example of modern, complex form that avoids the ubiquitous concrete and is created by the use of traditional techniques and materials.

South elevation with exposed steel frame supporting the wooden structure

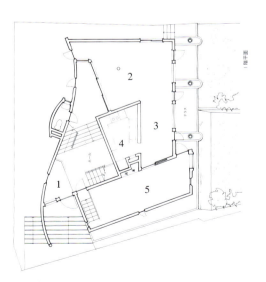

First floor plan   S = 1:250

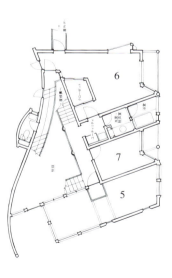

Second floor plan

Third floor plan

1 Entrance and hall
2 Living room
3 Dining place
4 Kitchen
5 Studio
6 Parents
7 Children
8 Storage room

Walls of clay finished with coloured lime

Terrace in front of the living room

Undulated clay wall, covering the half timber structure, finished with coloured lime plaster

Studio

Stair hall

MATSUZAKA WORKING WOMEN'S CENTER

Matsuzaka City, Mie Prefecture, 1985

Artificial ground, Hanging Corridor, Cubic 'Machiya'

The City of Matsuzaka, located in the same area as the Ise Shrines, is a typical castle town of post-medieval times. Much of the ancient city grid and many of the old buildings are still preserved, partly due to the fact that the city was not bombed during the last war.

Matsuzaka is also known as the home town of the Mitsui family which founded the Mitsui company in the Edo period and of Norinaga Motoori who was a famous scholar and a poet, also of the Edo era. Both can perhaps be seen as symbols of the wealth and of the culture of the town.

The house for the Working Women is thus a public facility planted right in the middle of a traditional urban environment and is just one of the facilities of a redevelopment plan aimed at making the existing environment more attractive, as well as bringing some vitality back to this commercial area.

In the times when the pilgrimage was still very popular in Japan, thousands of pilgrims would pass along the Ise highway which runs through this quarter with a width of only a few feet. One can only imagine how crowded it must have been with everybody walking toe to heel, as they say.

The merchants of the shopping street along the old Ise highway, 'Nakamachi-Shōtengai', are making redevelopment plans to revitalize the quarter. It is planned to make a promenade circulation along the centre stream and redevelop buildings by uniting several lots. There is also a parking area for people shopping, which is made of vacant lots after the rebuilding of old town houses. The merchants' cooperative intended to create a public facility above this parking site, to revitalize the street by gathering people together.

Thus it was decided to build the 'Matsuzaka Working Women's Center' managed by the Labour Administration Section of the City Government, which deals with working women's social problems, provides meeting rooms and holds seminars and cultural activities for working women, directly over the parking area.

We accepted the design from Matsuzaka city commission in early June 1985, and had to finish all the tender drawings by the middle of September. This short design period is a bad custom of public building, intended to achieve the completion of a building in a single budget year. We also had to solve the design problems under the many regulations of the redevelopment plan. We decided after studies on the three points below.

1. to make an artificial ground level on the second floor and to express this strongly, to give it the same condition as the ground, and avoid the sense that the building is on the parking area which has no relation to this facility.

2. to make a hanging corridor above and along the promenade on the south edge which will be set up after the reclamation of the water gutter at the edge. It will be an adaption of the traditional spatial order of the 'Machiya' (old town house) which has deep earth floor corridors.

3. not to spoil the sequence of the continuous row of 'Machiya' and to create a new model of the redevelopment form by reading the form, volume, section and system of 'Machiya'.

My 'Zoo' team in Kobe University had been making a comparative study of a variety of traditional house forms in and around Matsuzaka town, cooperating with Takamasa Yoshizaka of Waseda University and his team in 1979–1980. From this study we learned that the sizes and outlooks are different between classes of inhabitants, but there are some common features which are the spatial order and the land-use system in each strip-like site. The sectional order of the site of the houses of 'samurai' (warrior), 'chōnin' (townsfolk) and farmer are common and a conversion can be considered. We tried to learn and accept the spatial order from the traditional forms rather than to quote directly. Pitched roofs, roof tiles, and set back sections are adopted from the traditional spatial order, and artificial ground, hanging corridors, volume formation, void sections and small terraces are our conversion. In this way, a new cubic 'Machiya' appeared.

Tsutomu Shigemura

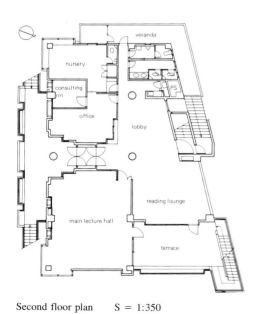

Second floor plan   S = 1:350

Third floor plan

Fourth floor plan

Reading lounge on the second floor

EXHIBITION OF JAPANESE ARCHITECTURE

Düsseldorf Stadtmuseum, 1983, Tsutomu Shigemura and Manfred Speidel

A corridor made up of red gates crossed the space and sank into a terraced mound, with light shining out from a crack. The mysterious Inari shrine in Kyoto, dedicated to the goddess of prosperity and her helpers, the foxes, was the motif around which the exhibition was arranged. Curved gravel surfaces designed according to the 18th century painter Sotatsu formed a dry river to complete the "landscape".

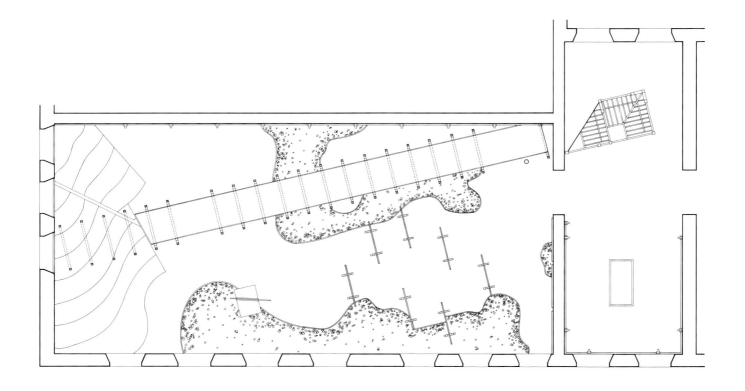

BRIDGE

1982

"Reincarnation Osaka" was the title of a series of architectural exhibitions mounted in 1982. The theme of the last of these exhibitions was "Bridges", based on a famous tragic love story called "Sonesaki Shinju".

The hero was a sober merchant, but he was deeply in debt through having spent all his money on love in the Geisha district of Osaka. Since he was unable to satisfy his creditors, the only way out of his dilemma seemed to be suicide. He walked with his lover from bridge to bridge – nine in all – then jumped into the river from the last one, the Tenma-Bashi bridge.

The Atelier Iruka was commissioned to design this last bridge. It had to mark the climax of the story, and so something unusual was needed, something absolutely original, something fantastic. As a result the bridge is organic in shape, to convey the erotic aura of the story.

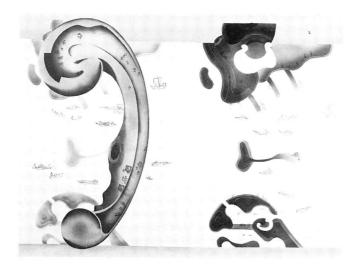 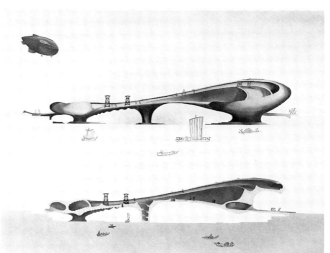

FLOWER AND GREEN

World Exposition, Osaka, 1990

The Bamboo-Dome. North Gate.
Laminated timber arches are covered with grids of bamboo grown over by plants. The span of the arches is 45 metres. The walls are filled and finished with earth.

The Gajumaru (Banyan Tree) North-West Gate.
Big steel structures are supporting a shading roof of bamboo. Plants grow at the pillars to cover the structure. Steel, timber, bamboo, plants, and clay walls are mixed. The circumference of the structures measures 25 metres. It covers two plazas, one for the entrance, the other for the resting-place.

The Bamboo-Dome

The Bamboo-Dome

The Gajumaru Gate

COMMON VILLAGE UTSUSE

Tada New Town, Kawanishi-City, Hyogo Prefecture, 1988–89

The steeply sloped site was what remained from a housing development. The developer (Seiyo Kankyo Kaihatsu) and we decided not to divide up the land. We gathered interested clients and produced with their participation a neighbourhood including common space and nature. The six houses have individual plans and shapes, the boundaries between are just lightly indicated by landscaping.

First floor plans

HONJO KINDERGARTEN

Honjo, Akita Prefecture 1975

This kindergarten in the little town of Honjo is located in a business area behind the station. Working parents leave children from babies to five-year-olds in the kindergarten during the day. It can accommodate up to 150 children. The children are organized in both mixed and similar age groups.

The closed rooms on the ground and upper floors are for same-age groups of three- to five-years-olds, and can also be used in pairs with a communal corridor between them for mixed groups. Infants play and sleep in the large room with the stairs in the upper storey. On the ground and upper floors there is a work-room for painting and one for potting between each pair of classrooms. On the ground floor a large group of rooms consisting of dining-hall, playroom and kitchen forms a structured whole. The kitchen is glazed, so that the children can look in and the staff can look out. The large rooms have multifunctional steps and rostra, offering varied play facilities for the children.

The dining-hall and waiting room at the entrance are used by local people for meetings. The undulating roof is adapted to the flow of the wind, just as the curved walls fit into the children's movements.

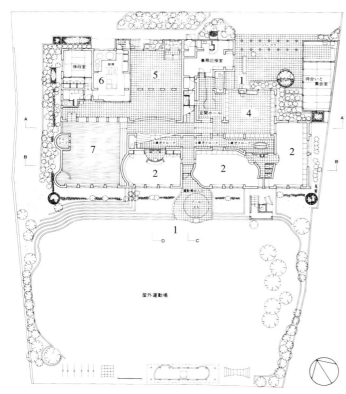

First floor plan   S = 1:500

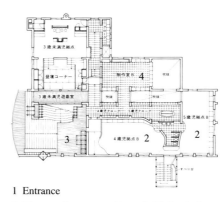

Second floor plan

1 Entrance

2 Three to five years old   5 Dining hall

3 Infants   6 Kitchen

4 Working rooms   7 Playroom

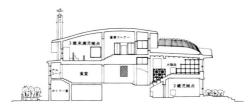

Entrance side from the street

View from the playroom of the infants (7) upstairs. To the left opens the dining hall.

The infants' playroom as double-stepped space

From upper part of the playroom towards the dining hall

TOKIWA KINDERGARTEN

Mizawa, Iwate Prefecture, 1983

This kindergarten accommodates 20 one- to two-year-old children and 70 three- to five-year-olds.

The extended entrance hall forms a link between play- and workrooms in the north, inner playground and dining hall with kitchen and offices to the east. The entrance building and catering wing are single-storeyed, and the roof is planted, and can be walked on. At the end of the play wing is a large hall, a hint of an amphitheatre let into the rectangle, and its steps lead to the upper storey on one side. In contrast with this large room with gym and stage facilities there is a miniature bay on the garden side, with little houses for sitting and playing outside in front of it.

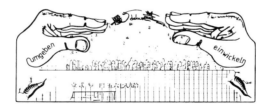

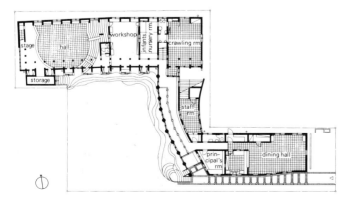

First floor plan   S = 1:600

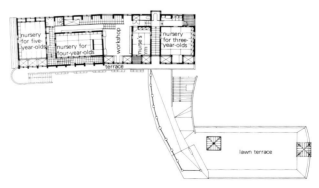

Second floor plan

80

Roof garden on the entrance building leading to the two storeyed nursery

Dining hall

Pavilion on the dining hall roof garden

Entrance passage

Hall

GOLF CLUB

Higashi Tsukuba, Ibaraki Prefecture, 1976

This is the second golf club designed by Atelier Mobile for the same client. "This time he wanted it in the English style. I did not know what that was, but I supposed it meant very lavish and full of panelling. I replied that I couldn't do English style but that I could create beautiful spaces."

This club was designed at the same time as the Nakijin community center, where the first project consisted of a series of poles topped with a framework. But in Nakijin the residents didn't want a the wooden frame, nor the tile covering, because of typhoons.

When the club was finished the client thought there were too many poles (there is 1.8 m between axes) but he felt that this made it seem very English.

Half the basement is intended for locker rooms and is covered with a roof in the form of waves planted with turf to minimize the impact of the building on its surroundings. The door handles represent animals: butterflies, snakes and fish, as a reminder of destroyed nature. There are five separate patios. Surface area: basement 1,751 sq. m, ground floor 1,327 sq. m.

Door handles

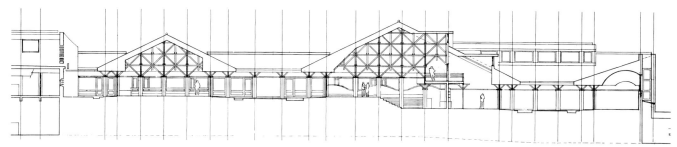

Longitudinal section

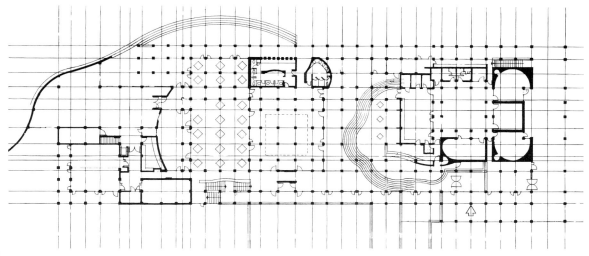

First floor plan

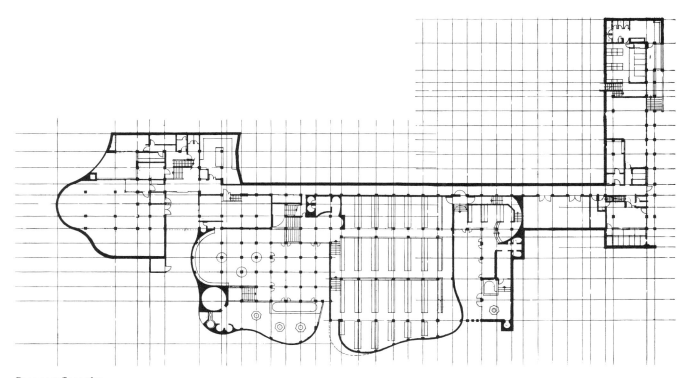

Basement floor plan

Planted roof above locker rooms with toplight-windows

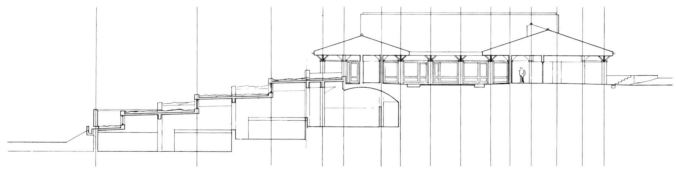

Cross section

87

UNDULATING MONSTER

Kaminokawa, Tochigi Prefecture, 1983–84

Kaminokawa is situated midway between Utsunomiya City and Oyama City. It was once a prosperous castle town, and is now known for its auto industry. Half of the townspeople are farmers who, on the side, work with robots in Nissan's Tochigi factory.

Here and there we can still see some very old trees which remind us of the past. They include podocarpus, holly, zelkova and Japanese nutmeg. Most of them are more than five hundred years old.

To the east is a well-known pottery town called Mashiko; to the west Tochigi City with rows of old houses, and to the south, Yūki City, famous for its graceful fabrics. To the north stands the exotic and world-famous shrine Toshogu, in the Nikko Mountains.

But the most typical features of Kaminokawa are the vinyl plastic of the greenhouses for gourds, 'Karaoke' (singing to taped accompaniment), dancing, and brand-new cars running through the farmlands. The greenhouses vary in shape and size, and the range of their frame arches is beautiful. The interior view of the tensional structure is especially impressive. The product of dried gourd shavings (or 'Kampyo', a material used in 'sushi') is the best in Japan. It is a wonderful sight to see spherical or pear-shaped gourds heaped along paths between fields.

The number of audio units for 'Karaoke' is also the highest in Japan. It is extraordinary to see so many people dress up and get together every night in 'Karaoke' bars surrounded by gourd fields. The war generation is especially enthusiastic about 'Karaoke'. They sing 'Enka' (mournful love songs) one after another on a spotlit stage and dance as if they wish to redeem the youth lost during wartime. They also have an unusual practice of buying their sons and daughters a good car to prevent them from missing out on Tokyo. Such high school educated sons and daughters equip their cars with very expensive audio components and luxurious carpets, and, as with their Japanese tatami rooms, never enter with their shoes on. It's really their private room on wheels, from which they watch the flowing white clouds of pear blossoms, candelabrum-like violet paulownia flowers, the numberless umbrellas of large gourd leaves, the private groves and the beautiful Nikko Mountains. In such scenery and with such customs, they cannot do without cars any longer.

A Social Hall

An important problem for a private enterprise from another city was how to establish commercial space that approximates a community center, and how to plant its roots in Kaminokawa soil where blood and territorial relationships are strong and public facilities are excellent.

The final plan was a 'townspeople's social hall' which had to be of easy access. It includes a room for drinks and light meals, rental rooms and halls for meetings, conferences, lectures and studytraining facilities. It also includes an open-air stage, lawns for dancing and 'Karaoke', and a children's playground.

Various Shapes and Forms

The open-air exhibit ground is surrounded by sasanqua windbreak trees to the north, a hundred-metres long Exhibition Hall to the south, an open-air stage on the east and a repair shop to the west. The approach through the 'Nagayamon' (farmer's house gate) which cuts across the Exhibition Hall leads along the wisteria and kiwi pergola in the open-air exhibition ground to the parking lot.

Reinforced concrete pillars on the second floor support girders and beams with their eighteen branches which shoot outwards from the five-coloured capital of each. The gourd- or wildcat-shaped roof is exposed to blasts of cold air which sweep down from Mt. Nantai (the highest peak in Nikko).

The Exhibition Hall has a row of square pillars along the south side gallery. The pillars are faced with Oya and Ashino stone, and each has its own pattern giving five different designs. The pedestal is of rough Tage stone, and the capital is hawk-and-pigeon-shaped with branches shooting out from its back. The pigeon, which also looks like a blue-and-white flycatcher (prefectural bird), is facing the clouds over Mt. Nantai and the Kinu River and has a gourd leaf instead of an olive branch in its beak. They are all made by Oya Village artisans. There is also a row of twelve cat-shaped weather-vanes in front of the pillars. Each 'weather-cat' holds a bird or fish or kampyo or a steering wheel in its paws. These are the work of the craftsmen of Mibu Village.

The ceiling of the Exhibition Hall is covered with stainless-steel panels which reflect colourful cars kaleidoscopically. On the parapet of the second floor, 300 cats in the scenery of Shimotsuke are painted in fresco style.

Insulation of the north tricolour wall, window frame insulation, double-glazing, floating floors and underfloor heating have been adopted.

Tomcats, tabbycats, tortoiseshell cats, kittens, grimalkins and all the other cats of the Exhibition Hall can therefore enjoy comfort – even during severe winters.

Rather than the cold space created by high-tech materials, warm spaces with various shapes and forms created by the skill of craftsmen have an appeal for almost everybody.

Cutting with Laser Beams

The large table in the second floor refreshment room is made of two different kinds of stone, pale green Tage and light grey Ashino. The chairs, triangular tables and cat-shaped lights are all cut by laser beam. Not only in this room, but also in many other parts of the main exhibition hall, are placed laser-cut objects, such as jardiniers, bracketed cat lamps on the walls, doorhandles with the wavy pattern of the Kinu River and a blue and white fly-

catcher. On the isosceles triangle table top, cats are depicted chasing mice. The small armchair is called by a girls' name, Hanako, and the big armchair by a boys', Taro. The wavy-shaped tables all fit together amusingly – rather like a jigsaw puzzle. Together with the intricate openwork patterns of the screens, all these objects are made of limewood ply and are cut by computer-programmed laser beams.

Over the last six years, Atelier Mobile has been testing laser beaming in cooperation with Atelier Hoenkan and UG Sato. Technical assistance was provided by Laser Craft Co. which had the original know-how in programmed beaming and cutting for printing perforation.

Kinya Maruyama

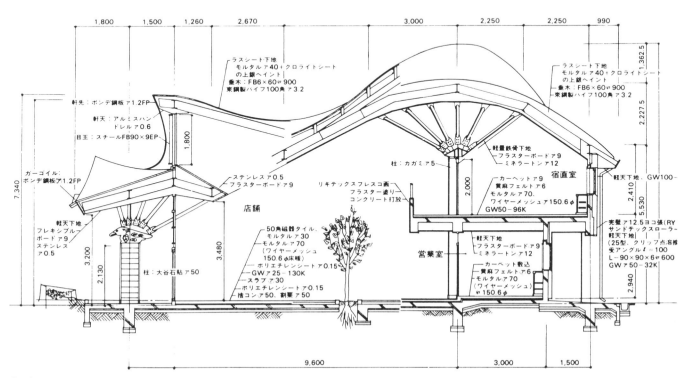

Section   S = 1:120

Undulating roof supported by steel pipes on pillars with bird-capitals

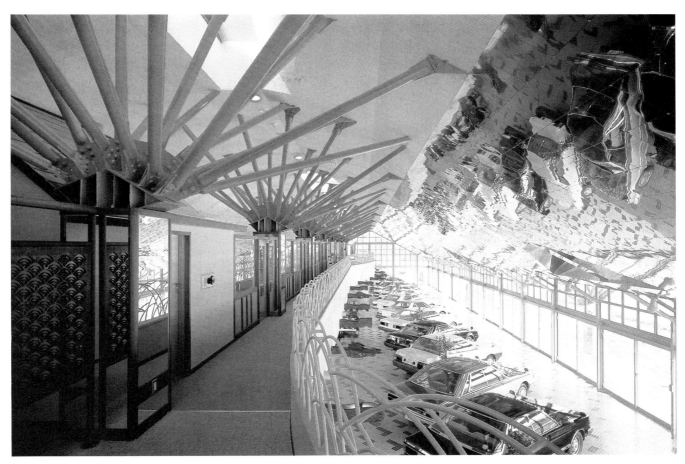

Showroom with stainless steel ceiling. Details of laser-cut panels on the left

FUJIMA FLATS

Kudan, Tokyo, 1980

Casa Fujima is a block of rented flats near Ichigaya station in Tokyo, in a small, quiet street between Kiyukuni Street and Ichigayabori Street. The area around the station is still largely residential, with a lot of green spaces, but the cityscape is gradually changing. Many small buildings have to make room for large blocks of rented flats and other residential buildings.

In front of the entrance to Casa Fujima is a little square, leading to the street like an alleyway. The building is bordered on the left by the large end wall of an office block, and the garden wall of a detached house on the right. The open entrance is intended to make the cool atmosphere of the neighbouring building less monotonous, more friendly. The entrance has a large protruding roof and is decorated with plants and flowers for the various seasons. It also serves as an entrance to the café on the ground floor. In summer the "entrance alley" is also a café terrace,

children's playground and evening meeting place for neighbours. This helps to create a peaceful atmosphere for passers-by.

Each flat has warm-water underfloor heating.

The small gate in the wall to the right of the building, the nameplates on the doors, door handles, post box, tables and chairs in the entrance hall and notice boards were crafted by a skilful carpenter, and make the entrance area a friendly and inviting place.

The facade is staggered in terrace form in two directions. Foliage plants are still being established on the side facade, which together with the lilac-striped pattern on the outer walls is intended to have a peaceful effect on passers-by. This is my wish.

Akiyoshi Okamura

Third floor plan with apartments

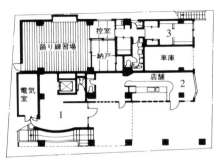

First floor plan   S = 1:400

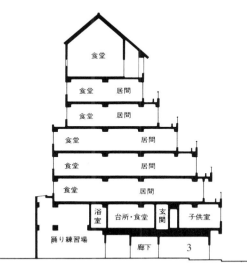

Section

1 Entrance hall
2 Café
3 School for Japanese dance

93

Entrance gate on the side

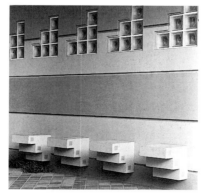

Outside wall of cafeteria

Entrance hall

SATO HOUSE

Kagurazaka, Tokyo, 1983

This is a graphic designer's house, and contains his studio.
Motifs from his pictures in the manner of Escher can be found in
and on the house: on the balcony rails these become pictures of
animals when seen from the side; others are used as imprints on
the concrete wall and as a wall jigsaw in the living room.
Plywood wall jigsaw and plywood furniture were designed and
produced by Laser Craft and Hoenkan.
The striking and apparently grotesque furniture is comfortable to
use.

Shinshukan. Council chairs, 1980 (Zō, Hoenkan, Endo Planning)

Shinshukan. Stools Child of Romeo and Juliet, 1980
(Zō, Hoenkan, Endo Planning)

The Quartering of a Circle
Furniture Design

Sometimes curious errors are made: as in *The Little Prince,* that famous story by Saint-Exupéry: of a design which at first sight appears to be a hat, but is disclosed to be a python that has swallowed an elephant.

This is exactly what happens in the world of Team Zoo designs. At first glance, just looking at their size and placement, one would never know them as pieces of furniture.

But, it is obvious, reality is first and above all, the true universe. One can be sufficiently convinced simply by looking: there are the rolling hills, there are the fish that swim up the stream, there are the trees filled with singing birds, the star-filled sky, a primeval forest, and there, the assembled geometric forms of a group that seems half submerged in a kind of fourth dimension. Irregular, embossed, pierced, eroded, pulpy, bloated, hunched, pointed, surprising, baffling, troubling; it does not try to break through the sound barrier, but succeeds in an incredible quartering of the circle, namely an unexpected mixture that is as miraculous as the obsessions of Gaudí and Mackintosh, those masters of design, who, exactly like Team Zoo, strove always to produce unique works that make their designs universal and beyond time and space.

Patrice Goulet

Sato House. Jigsaw-puzzle wall (Mobile)

Sato House (Mobile, Hoenkan)

Sato House. Taro chair, 1984 (Mobile, Hoenkan)

Zō, 1984

Mother chair, 1980 (Hoenkan)

Manhattan chair (Zō)

Shinshukan. Stools, 1980

Butterfly bench, 1986 (Mobile)

One and Another, 1986 (Mobile)

Manhattan chair (Zō)

Sato House. Omusubi chair, 1985
(Mobile, Hoenkan)

Zō, 1984

OKUSHITA RESIDENCE

Atami, Shizuoka Prefecture, 1985

The former Atami coast, with its memories of the white Sanoe and blue-green pines, sank into the Pacific Ocean long ago. The present Atami coast has been artifically shored up and reshaped. But Hatsushima Island, its praises sung in famous plays, still rises from the sea as it always did.

Almost all the buildings on the slope of Atami, including this house, are placed in a way that one has a splendid view of the island. You get off at Raigu station in the town of Jukkai, go past the great camphor tree at the Raigu temple in the direction of the park with the plum trees, then turn off right to the "ten countries pass" and suddenly come across the cloud-shaped terraces of the Okushita building bubbling up out of the earth.

The client had already commissioned summer houses and holiday facilities for his firm. This building is used as a holiday home for company employees. It is in two sections: two flats and a communal room. The flats are topped with curved gables and saddle roofs, and the community room is separated from them by a large terrace. Inside the room this takes the form of a funnel-shaped staircase, reflecting the topography. It is connected with the flats on ground-floor level. The staircase is a children's play area, and adults chat here, drink and sing. Coloured paper on walls and ceiling and lacquered lampshades stamped with constellations establish a peaceful, cheerful atmosphere.

Every room has a terrace with a splendid view of Hatsushima Island. The verdant green of the terraces protects the eye from the ugly multi-storey car park at the station and the neon lights of the Atami bathing area. The gables of the flats face the prevailing wind, making good ventilation possible. If you take the stairs, reminiscent of the inside of a barrel, down from the first floor to the ground floor, your eye is caught by the crumpled ricepaper ceiling, which reflects the sunlight mirrored in the sea.

The building still seems alien in its surroundings. I hope that some time its green terraces will get used to the valley and blend with the landscape.

G. Hasegaura

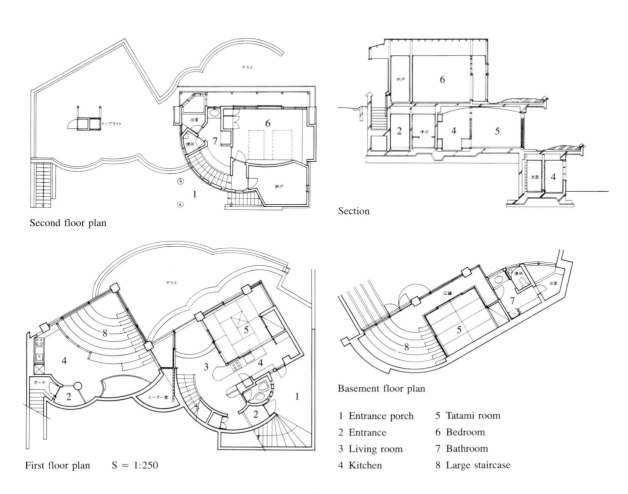

Second floor plan

Section

First floor plan   S = 1:250

Basement floor plan

1 Entrance porch	5 Tatami room
2 Entrance	6 Bedroom
3 Living room	7 Bathroom
4 Kitchen	8 Large staircase

View from the terraces towards the sea

Entrance porch

Funnel-shaped staircase as community room in the apartment to the left

Bedroom on the second floor

Living and tatami room on the first floor of the apartment to the right

L'AUTRE MAISON

Tatebayashi, Gumma Prefecture, 1985

Sixty kilometres north of Tokyo lies the city of Tatebayashi famous for its 'udon' (Japanese noodles). There a group of middle aged childhood friends with different occupations decided to have a small concert hall built for them. One of this group, Rieko Kaoi, acted as a producer and manager for this 'home ground' project. She said, their wish was to have good music performed, from traditional Japanese music to jazz and classical, in an environment where people in the community could communicate with each other harmoniously. They wanted to get away from the big impersonal halls like the ones built by the city authorities and opposed the tendency to consider Tokyo as the only center for the arts in Japan.

Looking around in Gumma Prefecture I was struck by the many vinyl hothouses, the rounded silhouettes of the zelkova trees and the way the northern winds cut across the land. This area is known for frequent floods, for supplying seasonal labourers (carpenters) for Tokyo, for pongee weaving, beautiful wheat mills, timber structures, Ōya stone warehouses and the still prevailing custom of using smoked-silvered roof tiles.

I wanted to combine these elements with my conception of enveloping light and sound to create a cheerful space that would be both relaxed and refreshing.

The hall is also used for a restaurant where you can have dinner to the tune of an old music box and while sitting at triangularshaped tables arranged in an arc. Drinks can be enjoyed from one of the many mushroom-like stools that spring from the walls, or from a three-legged chair with small table.

To build this furniture we used the wooden beams that belonged to the house that stood originally on this site, hoping that they will rejoice at this chance for a second life cycle.

The concrete walls are fiberglass insulated and covered by cedar clapboard. The roof is of the traditional smoked silvered tiles from the original house. These tiles were made in this area, allowing this hall to blend with the surrounding landscape.

On the inside the main wall is faced with Ōya stone (7 cm in width) and Ashino stone in traditional patterns. Other walls are simply done in unfinished plywood framing.

I am happy to say the performers and audience alike agreed on the quality of the acoustics and I think that is the result of a combination of architectural elements, high ceiling, sufficient volume, natural materials and cheerful furniture.

Music can make the atmosphere relaxing or stimulating, while the architecture and furniture also provide a peaceful and a lasting impression.

But, essentially I wanted to satisfy the desire for harmony expressed by this small community.

Kinya Maruyama

Hall during a concert

MILANO PENTHOUSE

Nakano-cho, Shinjuku-ku, Tokyo, 1986

This attic storey, known as "urban oasis", apparently conventional in its outward form in the shape of a Hokkaido barn roof, turns out to be a fairytale space inside, seeming to have been carved from the clouds.

Plywood trusses and taut ropes span the roof space, which in the daytime serves as the "Milano" fashion salon, and can be transformed into a party room at night. The plywood surfaces, like all Mobile's plywood work, are cut with laser beams.

Wooden animals with sparkling crystals spin before the windows as weathercocks.

All the furniture was designed by Mobile.

The tailor's salon

Sitting corner with a raised tatami floor

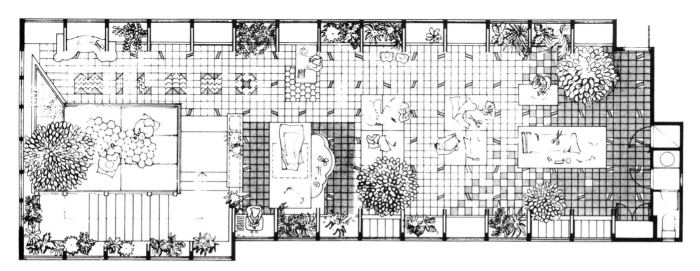

Floor plan

"Cloud" handles

Weathervane animals

HOUSE TAKITE

Shinagawa, Tokyo, 1987

The triangular house has been worked on over two and a half years with a conscious effort to create spaces of warmth and softness. In this high-tech city, Tokyo, such genuine architectural necessities could be dismissed as an old fashioned value. Takite was a creation based on the renunciation of the Modern movement. It is like a hand knit sweater, a casual and unpretentiously intimate world. Uneven tiles suffering from the cracks caused by disconnected mortar joints, rough plasterwork with a

tint of red sea-shell powder, and woodwork full of knots and crevices, reveal a lack of uniformity in the materials used as well as in the precision of the craftsmanship.

The open living room is defined by translucent shoji screens, a tatami bench from a cedar log, the tile floor with moravian accent tiles, and the large steps provided as a sitting place. In the middle a table in the shape of Mt. Fuji is accompanied by chairs decorated with small figures of animals.

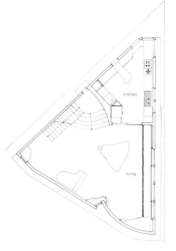

First floor plan   S = 1:250   Second floor plan   Third floor plan

Living room

Living room with Mt. Fuji table

PRINCIPLES OF DESIGN

Expression of Region

It is our desire that the architecture reflects the locality where it stands. We attempt to express the identity of the area or region in what we design. We walk around the village, survey the landscape, observe how people are living and investigate the local history. In this way we eventually uncover clues or keys for expressing the locality in our designs.

What is a House?
What is a School?
What is a City Hall?

We observe the basic living process of a community, a school or a family, and try to find the fundamental demands for the architecture that they plan to build. Sometimes the clients or community are not fully aware of their own wants or needs. It becomes a part of our work to think with them and to propose a plan for their new way of life. Our objective is to create spaces that answer the current demands of the client and community, while providing new opportunities to broaden the horizons of life.

Diversity

Architecture is an opportunity for various people to meet. Spaces affect how people make contact. Integrating spatial diversity into the structures presents a variety of environments where people can interact. By communicating diversity in form, materials and scale, we seek to develop in people using the architecture a sense of recognition and peace.

Emotional World

We design buildings to inspire an emotional response from the inhabitants. Upon entering our structures, people should experience some slight shock or stimulation of their five senses in order to alert them to the character of the space and its connection with the outside world.

The textures of materials and the forms we use within the space often represent the natural elements on the outside. Wind and water, sunlight and starlight, or a distant mountain view, are transmitted into the space in a very direct way. We utilize the organization of the space to activate the kinetic sense and impart the experience of time in a way that a soft, homogenous environment cannot. We feel strongly that the architecturally defined space should be a sensory experience.

Enhancing and Enjoying Nature

The structure and the space it defines impose a degree of control on the climate. To enjoy the climate there should be devices to soften the severe elements of heat, cold and humidity. Deep eaves, earth-covered roofs, wind passages and airwells are some of the softening devices we employ. The imperative of our design process is to search for balance between a mechanically controlled environment and nature in a building. Feeling hot or cold and being able to mark the changes of seasons within the structure is an important factor. From eons of living with nature, our bodies have evolved an internal awareness of the march of time. We want to design spaces that enhance our sensitivity to the events of the seasons, keeping the rhythm of our internal clock.

Aimai Moko and Jiku

It is our aim to create harmony between architecture and the environment. For that purpose we apply aimai moko and jiku.

First, aimai moko means that which is undefined, vague or ambiguous. An aimai moko space is by nature multi-functional and able to evoke various responses and moods. Such space serves to stimulate the imagination with an ambiance that is boundless, free-flowing and peaceful. As one example, to erase the division of inside and outside we provide aimai moko spaces as areas of transition. The porch, veranda, platform, eaves, piloti, open colonnade, arbor and trellis are elements we employ to create transition spaces. These spaces generate continuity in passing from outside to inside without an abrupt change of atmosphere. The spaces also serve to control sunlight and wind, rainfall and sound, while framing the view. Through these areas the community enters the building and the function of the building radiates into the community. People can meet here in their comings and goings and are provided with greater opportunities for communication. This is the "hand-shaking" point between the building and community.

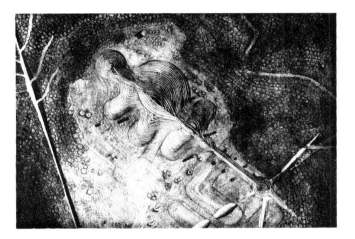

Second, we apply the traditional concept of jiku, which means axis. By using points of reference found in the natural landscape, the organization of the local town, celestial bodies or the changing of the seasons, we establish axes that converge on the site. From the layering of these geographical, celestial, directional, seasonal or urban axes, we select the orientation and capture the dynamic flow of the landscape and cosmos. The axes focus energy into the structure. Once we are inside the building, our imagination is propelled along the axes outward. Our purpose is to awaken people's sense of belonging to the cosmos.

Finally, the greening of the space with vegetation is most important.

NAGO CITY HALL

Nago City, Okinawa Prefecture, 1981 (In cooperation with Atelier Mobile)

The following points became the theme in order to give concrete answers to the subjects of a competition which were 'What is architecture in Okinawa?' and 'What is an ideal City Government Office?'

Seeking a new ideal state of city government offices

In order for a city government office to be truly open to its people, it must secure continuity with the daily life environment of the people who use it.

In this proposal there is a continuity between its interior and exterior, from the open space covered with grass to the lobby and office. The open space as well as the Asagi terraces on each floor are spaces which can be used anytime by anyone, and it's like a portion of the city which has come into the government office building.

Grasping the climate and natural features of Okinawa

It is necessary to grasp the temperature, humidity, intensity and direction of the wind, intensity of light, reflection of light and formation of shadows, not just as data but also with your body.

You can discover devices and wisdom for creating a comfortable environment when you are walking through the town. It is important to utilize them skilfully in the buildings. In this proposal devices are shading with Asagi-type louvers and pierced block screens, insulation with earth on the top floor, ventilation and dispersal of heat by wind passage. These are all utilizations of the resources of the region.

Expressing the qualities of Okinawa

Rural villages and cities are composed with materials such as concrete blocks, earth, trees and green spaces. Projecting this mixture of qualities was considered in the proposal. Concrete blocks, which spread at an enormous speed after the war, were used as the main material, and their various applications were considered. Concrete technology is extremely advanced, and blocks for pillars, decorative pierced blocks and fair-faced blocks were feasible because of this technical development.

Since its completion, this city government office has been functioning as the base for local autonomy in its true sense, and has blended with the scenery.

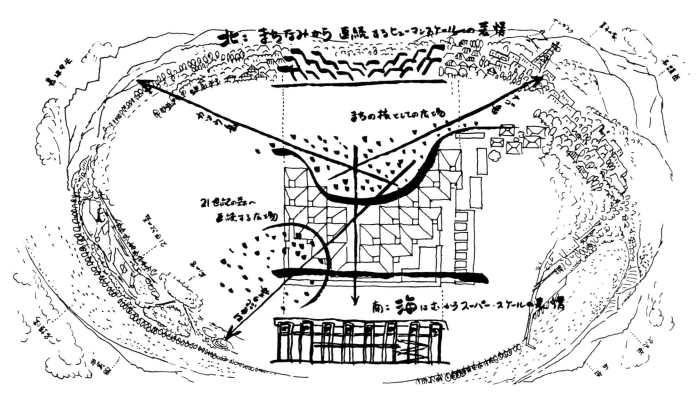

Large-scale front facing the sea, small-scaled terraces and roofs forming a plaza towards the community

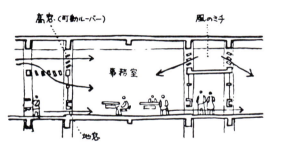

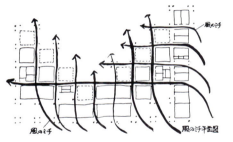

Using the wind from the sea for natural air-conditioning through large channels

1 Lobby
2 Board of education
3 Social welfare
4 Accounting section
5 Office space
6 Technical service rooms
7 Staff dining and rest
8 Mayor's room
9 Conference hall
10 Council rooms
11 Meeting rooms
12 Parking
13 Asagi terrace
14 Roof terrace with lawn

Third floor plan

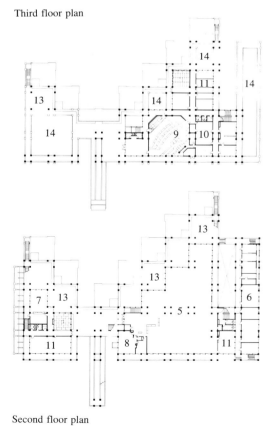

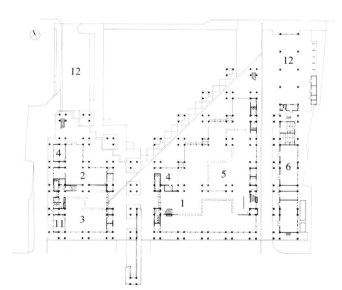

First floor plan   S = 1:500

Second floor plan

Asagi terrace and shadow roofs

Roof garden, view towards the sea

Concrete block structure and roof garden

ASACHO COMMUNITY CENTER

Asacho Imuro, Hiroshima Prefecture, 1985

Asacho Imuro is a town with old Kimachi tile roofs and is surrounded by stone terraced fields. It is located north of Hiroshima City, within a thirty minute drive from the downtown along the Ohta River. Resisting the overwhelming urban sprawl of Hiroshima to suburban rural communities, Asacho Agricultural Cooperative Association completed the construction of 'Co-op Town Asahigaoka'. The community was looking for a construction to serve as a place to represent the community such as villages and towns used to have in the past. It was sometimes a scene of a village shrine in a forest where people sat in a circle and drank together, with sacred music played on an outdoor stage, with roof tiles or natural stone masonry. Due to the strong demand from the president of the cooperative to build a domed building instead of a box-shaped one, we suggested the following. "A community hall is a small town, and it consists of a plaza with houses and terraced fields surrounding it and a dome covering it."

Section

1 Entrance

2 Stage

3 Main hall

4 Reception room

5 Office

6, 7 Back stage

8 Machine room

9 Storage

10 Women's study room

11 Small hall

12 Tatami room

13 Balcony

14 Terrace

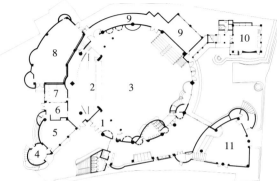

First floor plan   S = 1:1000

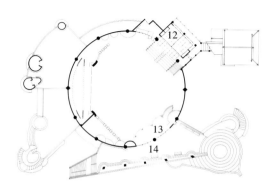

Second floor plan

With regard to the roofing tiles for the dome of 10 and some metres, a model was made to study the roofing details. The basic policy was to use generally available products. Everyone was enthusiastic because it was the first project in Japan to put Japanese tiles over a domed roof. Gargoyles with twelve horary signs and various trimming roof tiles were produced.

The proscenium arch's surface is of a *stucco lustro* finish by Akira Kusumi, a plasterer in Awaji. The soft luster has an overwhelming presence amidst the paint finish.

Natural stones were used for the exterior. According to the workers at the site whom I have talked with, the natural stones that can be used for masonry purposes are getting scarce. Having no other alternative, mountain rocks for Kenchi masonry were broken and chiselled to resemble the natural stones, and used in their place. I am hoping that moss will eventually grow on them.

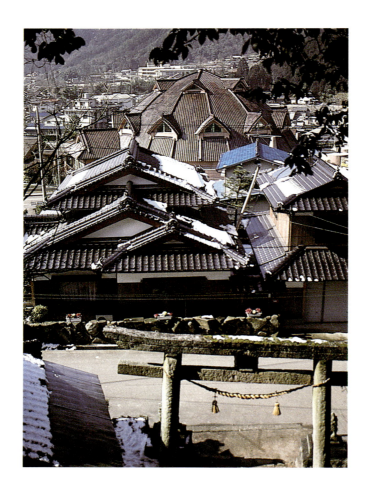

Stone stairway around reception room

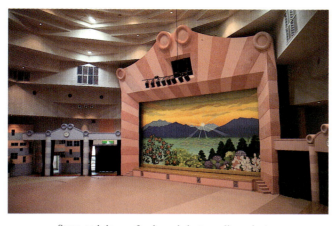 

Stage and dome of coloured, lustrous lime-plaster

The hall is like a plaza of a town

TOKUDA RESIDENCE

Natsumidai, Funabashi, Chiba Prefecture, 1986

Once in a while, when we visit land for designing, we get wrapped up in the dense and rich air. At that time, we are moved by the accumulation of lives that are etched in the ground and are possessed by the spirits that reside there.

The house is located on the edge of a plateau, spread out on top of a twenty metres high cliff that overlooks the city of Funabashi, which was once covered by the ocean. This plateau has been the site of many excavations which have unearthed such ancient things as pit dwellings and tombs. Using these fragments of old memories as clues, we can try to visualize what life was like on the plateau long ago. From among these visions, perhaps we can vaguely draw some idea of what the homes and lives will be like in the future. The homes and houses will probably be something like the following:

The house will be in unison with the passage of time and the changing of the seasons.
It will make one conscious of the memories of the land.
It will be a home where one can engrave one's own lifestyle on the land.
And that home will be like the following:
Abundant flowers and trees
The wind and the light can always be felt
A closeness to the stars, the clouds, and the birds
Goods and materials are abundant and diverse
Places other than simply rooms can be made
The boundaries will be discrete and unobtrusive
It will be a home where the residents can discover their own individual way to live as they choose.

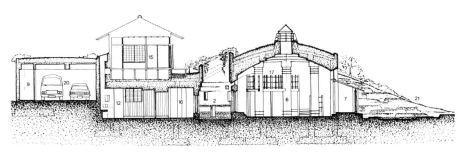

Section

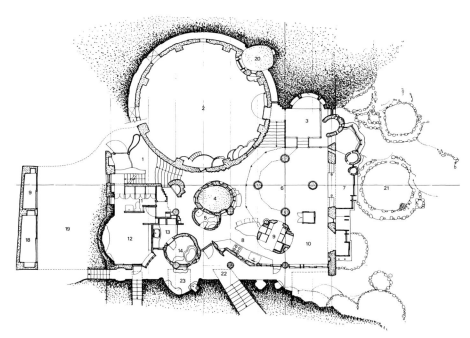

First floor plan   S = 1:300

1 Entrance
2 Sports room
3 Library
4 Courtyard
5 Lavatory
6 Living room: plaza
7 Wintergarden
8 Kitchen
9 Storage
10 Children's corner
11 Wardrobe
12 Bedroom
13, 14 Bathroom
15 Tatami room, teahouse
16 Passage
17 Gallery
18 Machine room
19, 20 Car port
21 Raised garden
22 Back entrance
23 Well

Tatami room – teahouse facing the roof garden

The open and glazed side of the cave-like house

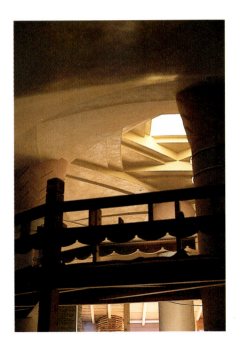

The concrete structure is clad with wood
which is covered by clay.

The finish is coloured and polished lime-plaster,
developed by Akira Kusumi

The plaza of the living room with
gallery and top light

Entrance   Window structure in the sports room

From cave to light and open space

KASAHARA MUNICIPAL ELEMENTARY SCHOOL

Miyashiro-cho, Saitama Prefecture, 1982

Miyashiro-cho of Saitama Prefecture is located exactly in the centre of the Kanto Plain. Within this characteristic scenery of the Kanto Plain that contains such rural features as rows of trees surrounding old mansions, rice paddies, the Tone River and vineyards, high voltage electrical towers along with groups of prefabricated homes are to be seen everywhere.

The waves and waves of rice paddies are just like a sea of green. There are also plantations looming in the distance. Small creatures can be seen in the irrigation ditches.

It is as if one scene gets divided into many smaller sights and they somehow manage to stir our memories. Logic makes all kinds of phenomena abstract, and as I go about erecting structures, I gather together all the fragments of images I have, etch them on my mind and hope that I can keep them in my heart.

The School is a City by Itself

A school is a little city within a big city. There are mountains, hills, ponds and roads with tall roofs overlapping smaller roofs. In the shade of a summer's day or in the depth of winter, the outdoor classrooms, the cafeteria and everything else in the school are places for interaction as well as places for learning. The classrooms, which are positioned so that they are surrounding the central garden, give one a sense of unification that is found in a small town. The music rooms, library, science labs, and industrial arts areas are located around the back garden. They seem to welcome the people of the city as they look out towards it.

The School is a Home

For young children, the school is indeed a second home. A small gabled roof forms the entranceway. Small alleys run out from each of the classrooms into the outer sidewalk just like the narrow pathways that run between houses. Each of the places has a designated name, for example, here is the train station and here is the train. As everyone gets on the train, they have group discussions, games, reading, and displays. Each person brings something from their own classroom. Then as other people pass by, the group gets larger and before long the whole school is involved.

On the opposite side of the talking area, near the windows, is an arts and crafts table with a sink which is used for a wide variety of projects. From here, there is an additional arts and crafts area that one can get to by going through the terrace and back garden. The fittings of the floors and walls of the classrooms are made of wood and there is plenty of space. In fact, there is enough area in the classrooms to accommodate times when two classes are having a lecture in the same room or if one class happens to be unusually large.

In the building containing the younger students, each room has its own separate outer door so that it can be opened to the central garden at any time.

The School is Full of Memories

The school has the appearance of a community with rows of trees merging into a two-storey tile-roofed building. Things like etching our names and notes on posters or poles near the school, looking up in the sky and seeing the various constellations, fields of butterflies, hanging decorations down from the tiles on the roof, the glass pictures that we made all by ourselves, the talking corner, and the daily washing of our feet with our best friends; these are the things that make up the memories of our younger years.

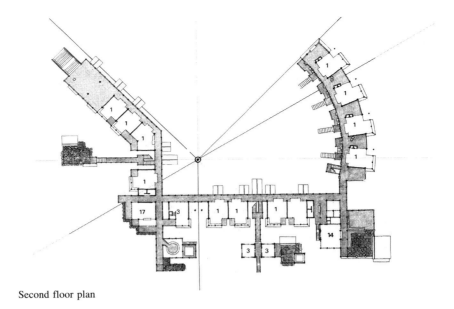

Second floor plan

1 Classroom
2 Tatami room
3 Faculty room
4 Music classroom
5, 6 Library
7 Dispensary
8 Science classroom
9 Preparatory room
10, 11 Art classroom
12, 13 Auditorium
14 Home sciences
15 Storage
16 Machine room
17 Meeting room
18 Grove
19 Outdoor theatre
20 Mt. Lunch
21 Mt. Rake
22 Farm
23 Courtyard
24 Play-pond "Jab-Jab"
25 Sports ground
26 Wisteria trellis

First floor plan   S = 1:400

Elder children's classrooms

Transition spaces from the garden
to the open corridors

The bay windows of a classroom open to the corridor like in an old town to the street

Entrance houses serve as transition spaces where street shoes are left

Small children's classrooms

Small huts and bay windows make the school into a small town

SHINSHUKAN COMMUNITY CENTER

Miyashiro-cho, Saitama Prefecture, 1980

I can recall what the people said about their experiences when they visited Shinshukan. "I can feel a kind of energy . . . The kind of energy that comes from a group." Among all the works of Atelier Zō, the Shinshukan is the foremost example of a structure where people from various places and in various ways participated in the design. Also, it was constructed with several different viewpoints in mind.

In considering the structure of the building, one must first stroll throughout the town, observing the people and the surroundings. Even more than that, the observations must broaden to the Kanto Plain, then Japan as a whole, and finally, the world. For each of these observations, one must try to analyze what forms and shapes are the most appropriate. The process starts with each piece of furniture and then broadens to include the entire structure.

The Atelier Zō members have appeared at many meetings and have made many new acquaintances and have concentrated their efforts on creating the Shinshukan. The reason that this large number of members did not become a disorganized crowd, but converged into a single large unit, is because they managed to find a few key phrases that they came up with in discussions. These important thoughts proved to be the major impulse in pursuing the ideal shape and form. The list of key phrases is:

Trees should be planted and the surrounding area should be made as green as possible.

The building should have a friendly atmosphere.

The building must be completed, even if it takes a long time.

The building must be multi-functional.

The building should express the local and regional flavour.

The form of the building should be fresh and unique.

The preceding key phrases came forth during the time progress was being made on the building as well as in the discussions. Certain individuals would meet with other individuals and the works and the discussions would be evaluated over and over. Eventually, little by little, we began definitely to secure a real feeling about what we wanted. However, a work that grasps exactly what we are feeling is truly hard work. The energy that each person was pouring into the effort began to be transferred into the work's shape and form.

If one can indeed feel the energy of the Shinshukan, or maybe the energy of a group of people, it must be the result of the enthusiasm (or maybe passion) of the people who actually participated in the construction. That is, the shape and form that resulted from their labour is what gives the work its deep feeling.

Entrance Passage

1, 2, 7 Entrance passage

3, 27, 28 Small hall

6 Corridor

8, 13, 14 Technical services

15 Lavatory

16–19 Tea-ceremony rooms

22, 23 Main hall

20, 30 Skylight, void

29 Colonnade

31, 32, 33 Children's library

35–38 Technical rooms and upper part of large hall

39 Terrace

40 Lawn plaza

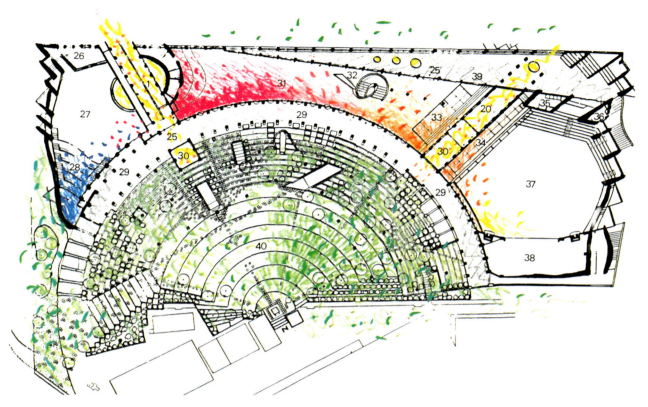

Second floor plan

First floor plan   S = 1:500

Skylight

Small hall for the meetings of the city council

The "hall" with brook and bridges

The "gallery" with a brook

The "salon" with a spring

The "salon"

Ornamental roof tile: a demon used as lamp

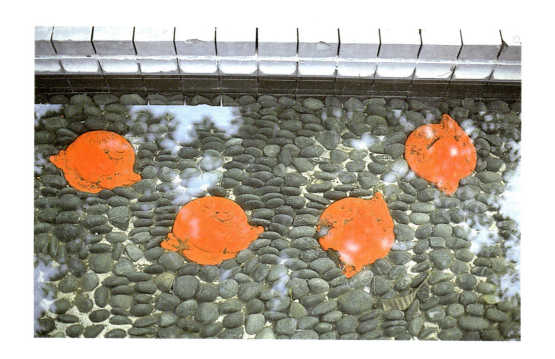

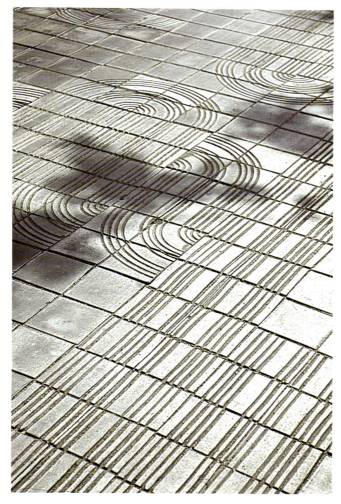

Tiles and ornaments

145